Date Due

THE REJECTED

THE REJECTED

Sketches of the 26 Men
Nominated for the Supreme Court
but Not Confirmed by the Senate

by
J. Myron Jacobstein
and
Roy M. Mersky

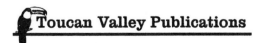

Toucan Valley Publications

Copyright © 1993 by Toucan Valley Publications
Cover photo courtesy of the collection of the Supreme Court
of the United States.

Library of Congress Cataloging-in-Publication Data

Jacobstein, J. Myron.
   The rejected : sketches of the 26 men nominated for the Supreme
Court but not confirmed by the Senate / by J. Myron Jacobstein and Roy
M. Mersky. -- 1st ed.
      188 p.   cm.
   Includes bibliographical references.
   ISBN 0-9634017-4-2
      1. Judges--United States--Selection and appointment--History.
2. United States. Supreme Court--Officials and employees--Selection and
appointment--History. 3. United States. Congress. Senate--History.
4. United States--Politics and government.   I. Mersky, Roy M. II. Title.
KF8776.J33   1993
347.73'2634--dc20
[347.3073534]   93-22374
                                              CIP

Manufactured in the United States of America
First Edition

CONTENTS

NOMINATIONS BY PRESIDENT

Chapter One

INTRODUCTION

Article II,Sec.2(2) of the United States Constitution provides that the President " . . . shall nominate, and by and with the advice and consent of the Senate, shall appoint . . . judges of the Supreme Court . . ."

In the 203 years between 1789 and 1992, Presidents have made twenty nominations for Chief Justice and 119 for Associate Justice, for a total of 139 nominations to the Supreme Court of the United States. Six of these nominees declined the appointment after being confirmed by the Senate. Of the remaining 133, twenty-seven (or twenty per cent) were denied confirmation by the Senate.

These *Sketches* will include the twenty-six men, one of whom was nominated twice, who would have accepted their appointments if they had been confirmed by the Senate. In addition to bringing the sketches of these individuals together in one volume, *The Rejected* also provides a snapshot of the issues that were dividing the country at the times of their appointments.

There is a voluminous literature on the Supreme Court and its Justices. A bibliography published by F. Martin and R. Goehaart in 1990 contains over 590 pages. Very little, however, has been written about those who were rejected by the Senate. What does exist is in books long out of print, or scattered throughout the pages of numerous periodicals.

Although recent appointments have received much publicity in the news media, such was not the case for most of the Presidential nominees of Supreme Court justices during the nineteenth century and the first quarter of the twentieth century. Until 1929, the Senate sat in closed sessions while considering all Presidential nominees, and not until the same year did the Judiciary committee call nominees to appear before it. Consequently, for most of the nominees in these sketches there are no official records of the Judiciary Committee Hearings or the debates in the Senate.

But there are sufficient secondary sources to reveal that the difficulties recent Presidents have had with obtaining Senate confirmation is not a new phenomena. Beginning with George Washington, sixteen Presidents out of thirty-nine had one or more of their Supreme Court nominees rejected by the Senate. Some recent appointments have been contentious and have received extensive television coverage of the Hearings before the Senate Judiciary Committee. Media commentators have lamented the personal attacks on the nominees, and that politics rather than qualifications now influence Presidential appointments. These *Sketches*, however, will reveal that attacks on the character of a nominee and scurrilous name-calling are not of recent origin. For better or worse, such practices started during the Presidency of John Adams, our second President, and have continued during the Presidencies of many of his successors.

As these *Sketches* are intended for the general reader and not for the legal scholar, we have omitted footnotes. Those interested in more comprehensive information about the events covered in these *Sketches* may consult Appendix II where the main sources consulted for this work are listed.

Chapter Two

President George Washington
1st President (1789-1797)
Party affiliation: Federalist

Supreme Court nomination not confirmed
by the United States Senate:

JOHN RUTLEDGE
Born: September 1739
Died: July 18, 1800
Education: Middle Temple, England
Appointed Associate Justice,
    September 24, 1789
    Resigned, March 5, 1791
Nominated Chief Justice,
    July 1, 1795
Rejected by Senate,
    December 15, 1795

5

When the First Congress of the newly-formed United States convened in Philadelphia in September 1789, one of the laws passed was the Judiciary Act of 1789 providing for a Chief Justice and five Associate Justices to form a Supreme Court. On September 24, President Washington nominated John Jay for Chief Justice and John Rutledge as one of the five Associate Justices. All six of President Washington's nominees were confirmed by the Senate on September 29, 1789, in accordance with the provisions of the Constitution.

John Rutledge was one of our "Founding Fathers." While practicing law in Charleston, South Carolina, he became active in politics and in the many events leading to the Declaration of Independence by the American Colonies. He participated in the Stamp Act Congress of 1765 and had membership in both the First and Second Continental Congresses of 1765. He was also elected in 1787 to the Federal Convention, convened to amend the Articles of Confederation but which instead drafted our present Constitution. A year after his confirmation he resigned from the Supreme Court in order to become Chief Justice of South Carolina.

In 1794, President Washington sent Chief Justice John Jay to England to negotiate a treaty that would settle several matters

7

that were in dispute between the two countries. When news of the proposed treaty became known in this country, it created quite a furor. Many felt that the terms of the treaty unfairly favored England. The dissent to the Jay Treaty was especially prevalent in the Southern states. On July 16, 1795, there was a large protest meeting against the treaty held at Charleston, South Carolina. John Rutledge was one of the speakers and in no uncertain terms he expressed his displeasure with the treaty.

Shortly before the Jay Treaty was published in the United States, John Jay was elected Governor of the State of New York and he resigned his position as Chief Justice effective July 1, 1795. Anticipating Jay's resignation, Rutledge sent a letter to President Washington indicating his willingness to accept the position of Chief Justice if it were offered to him. Washington did appoint him as Chief Justice effective July 1, 1795. The appointment came as a surprise to the public and probably to the sitting Associate Justices, who most likely assumed that the appointment would be made from among them. In a letter to James Monroe, Thomas Jefferson wrote that "[Rutledge's] appointment . . . seems to have been intended merely to establish a precedent against the descent of that office by seniority and to keep five mouths always gaping for one sugar plum."

It should be kept in mind that in those days communications were very slow; there were no telephones, telegraphs, or fax machines and it is not clear whether Rutledge received the information about his nomination before or after his Charleston speech against the Jay Treaty. In any case, when his speech was published in the Northern newspapers, it created a sensation, with a clamor arising against his confirmation.

As the Senate was not to meet until December 1, 1795, Rutledge served as Chief Justice under an interim appointment of the President. When the Senate convened in December, it had before it the matter of whether or not to confirm Rutledge as Chief Justice. Although there was some support expressed for his confirmation, there was also much opposition. One prominent person noted that however disagreeable it may be to suggest an error in the judgment of the President, it was to be hoped that Rutledge would not be confirmed. A prominent Federalist wrote to Alexander Hamilton: "To my astonishment I am recently told that John Rutledge has had the tender of the office of Chief Justice. By the favor of Heaven the commission is not tendered and I now presume it will not be!" Hamilton replied: "I find it is true that John Rutledge has been invited to become Chief Justice, but he is not commissioned, and I must presume he will not be after his late conduct."

On December 15, the Senate did vote fourteen to ten not to confirm. Thus, the Senate for the first time, acting under the Advice and Consent clause of the Constitution, used its power to reject a President's nominee for the Supreme Court. This caused Thomas Jefferson to write: "The rejection of Rutledge by the Senate is a bold thing, for they cannot pretend any objection to him but his disapprobation of the Treaty. It is, of course, a declaration that they will receive none but tories [sic] hereafter into any Department of the government."

In his *Supreme Court in United States History*, Charles Warren noted:

> The rejection of Rutledge was an event of great importance in American legal history, which hitherto received cursory attention. But for his unfortunate Charleston speech he undoubtedly would have been confirmed. . . . As his death did not occur until the year 1800, the Chief

Justiceship . . . would have become vacant at a time when it is extremely unlikely that President Adams would have appointed John Marshall as his successor. Thus upon the event of one chance speech regarding a British treaty hinged the future course of American constitutional law.

Upon the rejection of Rutledge by the Senate, President Washington nominated Associate Justice William Cushing as Chief Justice, but he declined the nomination. The President then nominated Oliver Ellsworth. Ellsworth was confirmed by the Senate as the Chief Justice of the Supreme Court of the United States.

Chapter Three

President James Madison
4th President (1809-1817)
Party affiliation: Democratic-Republican

Supreme Court nomination not confirmed
by the United States Senate:

ALEXANDER WOLCOTT
Born: September 15, 1758
Died: June 16, 1828
Education: Yale College
Read law in law office
Nominated Associate Justice,
February 4, 1811
Rejected by Senate,
February 13, 1811

When James Madison became President in 1809, the country was facing serious economic problems. These were caused primarily by the Embargo Act enacted during the second term of President Jefferson. At the time, France and England were at war and the English navy was intercepting and capturing American ships sailing for France. The Embargo Act prohibited all commerce by the United States between France and England. It was hoped that this Act would hurt England's economy and force it to stop its interference with American ships. It did little harm to England, however, but greatly damaged the economy of the United States, especially the New England states. During the first year of Madison's term, the Embargo Act was repealed and replaced by the Non-Intercourse Act which prohibited commerce between England and France unless they agreed not to harass American shipping. As neither country agreed, the Non-Intercourse Act continued to harm the American economy.

Other important issues were also being considered by Congress, and were strongly opposed by some and strongly favored by others. One hotly debated issue was whether or not a national bank should be established. Another concerned whether monopolies should be granted to companies using the recently invented river steamboats.

When Justice Cushing died in 1811, President Madison had his first opportunity to make a Supreme Court appointment. For the first time, the Supreme Court claimed a place in the national interest as it was realized that the Court would have the final say on the many important issues under consideration and that the new Justice would probably have the deciding vote on many of these issues. The Court at this time consisted of three Federalist Justices (Marshall, Chase, and Washington) and three Republican Justices (Johnson, Iredell, and Livingston). Thus the person appointed to replace Cushing could influence the future trends of the Court.

Madison first offered the nomination to Levi Lincoln, Attorney-General under President Jefferson and a former Governor of Massachusetts. But after a long delay, Lincoln declined due to his ill health.

Madison then considered nominating Joseph Story but rejected him because of his young age of thirty-one and the advice he had received that Story had Tory sympathies. Instead, on February 4 he astonished the nation by appointing Alexander Wolcott.

Wolcott was born in Winsor, Connecticut. After he was admitted to the Bar, he settled there to practice law but later moved to Middletown. In 1801, President Jefferson appointed him Collector of the Port, a position he held for many years. The Embargo Act and the subsequent Non-Intercourse Act placed the enforcement of these Acts on the Collector of the Port, a position often given by the President as a "political plum." In this position Wolcott was essentially a tax collector, and public opinion, then as now, has seldom held such persons in high regard. In the case of Wolcott, his lack of judicial experience combined with his duties in enforcing the custom laws caused him to have many enemies, especially among the Northern merchants.

New England newspapers immediately gave voice for those discontented with Wolcott's Supreme Court nomination. *The National Intelligencer* wrote that "[t]o nominate so hated a man for the Supreme Court with testimonials to his judicial fitness was [a] first rate political blunder." The *Columbian Centinel* on February 16 contained a dispatch from a Washington correspondent who wrote: ". . . even those most acquainted with modern degenracy [sic] were astonished at this abominable nomination. . . ."

In the *Connecticut Courant,* another Washington correspondent in a dispatch dated February 7 wrote:

On Monday the 4th, the President of the United States *nominated* ALEXANDER WOLCOTT, Esq. of Middletown in this state, *a Judge of the Supreme Court of the United States,* in the room of the Hon. Wm. Cushing 'deceased.' For about ten years has this man been fattening upon an office, the emoluments of which were derived solely from commerce. Yet such is his hostility to the merchants, or such his devotion *to the Continential System of Napoleon,* that in a public place in this city, a short time since, he remarked that the merchants of this country had governed it long enough, *that they must be put down,* that every man who owns a part of a sloop or a hogshead of molassess, undertook to dictate measures for the government; but Congress were of his opinion *the merchants might all go to hell in their way,* and that the non-intercourse laws would

be rigorously enforced . . . let the consequences
to the merchants be what they may.

Similar opinions about Wolcott were also published in
many other newspapers. The *New York Evening Post* for
February 20, 1811, carried three comments from other
newspapers. These were:

It gives me peculiar satisfaction to inform you,
that the Senate have this day rejected the
nomination of Alexander Wolcott as an Associate
Judge of the Supreme Court of the United States.
The vote was 24 against 9. The independence of
executive influence, and the disposition, to
enquire, have in this instance, been very honorable
to the Senate. *Conn. Ad.*

It is said that the Senate will not agree to the
nomination of Alexander Wolcott as Judge in the
place of Judge Cushing; his private character
being so bad. . . . There is some virtue in the
majority of the Senate. Wolcott is said to be . . .
more fit by far to be arraigned at the Bar than to
sit as a Judge. *Virg. Pat.*

It was once thought that candidate for the office of
judge of the highest court of law, should be a man
of learning, particularly in the science of law, that
he should be possessed of a fair character for
integrity, honesty and morality - that he should be
free from gross vices and vindictive passion. . . .
It was also once thought, that such a candidate
should not be possessed of low vulgar manners,
and habituated to conversation which would

become billingsgate and the brothel. *Con. Mir.*

Even those in favor of Wolcott's nomination, such as Levi Lincoln who called attention to his "larger mind, greater perception, and discriminatory powers," could find little favorable to say about his legal ability.

On February 13, 1811, the Senate voted twenty-four to nine not to confirm Alexander Wolcott, despite the fact that President Madison's party had a large majority in the Senate.

History has confirmed the wisdom of the Senate in its refusal to confirm Wolcott. Richard J. Purcell in his *History of Connecticut* relates how several years after Wolcott's rejection by the Senate, he was a delegate to the Convention considering a new Constitution for Connecticut. There he voiced the opinion that any judge declaring a law unconstitutional should be expelled as exercising usurped power. The Supreme Court in the early nineteenth century was developing the right of judicial review of congressional laws. It may well have had difficulties in so doing if Wolcott had been on the Supreme Court and had continued to believe that judges did not have the power to hold certain laws unconstitutional. Moreover, in place of Wolcott President Madison nominated Joseph Story, a prominent attorney, who was quickly confirmed by the Senate and served for thirty-four years. Court historians now rate him as one of the all-time great Supreme Court Justices.

The failure of the Senate to confirm Alexander Wolcott foreshadowed what future nominees might face as politics continued to play an important role in presidential appointments of Supreme Court Justices.

Chapter Four

President John Quincy Adams
6th President (1825-1829)
Party affiliation: Democratic-Republican

Supreme Court nomination not confirmed
by the United States Senate:

JOHN J. CRITTENDEN
Born: September 10, 1787
Died: July 26, 1863
Education: Washington College
(now Washington and Lee);
William and Mary College
Nominated Associate Justice,
December 17, 1828
Postponed, February 12, 1829

During the terms of President James Monroe (1817-1825) the mood of the country became known as the "Era of Good Feeling." But by the end of his administration, this mood had changed and the country was divided by both political and geographical differences. This was reflected in the election of 1824 where there were four candidates: John Quincy Adams, Henry Clay, William Crawford, and Andrew Jackson. None of these candidates received a majority of the Electoral College votes and as provided for by the Constitution, the election had to be decided by the House of Representatives with each state having but one vote. By a narrow margin, John Quincy Adams was elected President of the United States.

In 1828, Adams ran for reelection but was defeated by Andrew Jackson. In those days the Constitution provided for the election in November, with the inauguration not taking place until the following March. Also, the new Congress convened in December after the November election. The incumbent President thus had several months serving as a "lame duck" President. In December 1828, Associate Justice Robert Trimble died. Adams offered to nominate Henry Clay, but Clay declined and strongly recommended to President Adams that John Crittenden, a prominent Kentucky lawyer, be nominated.

21

In a letter to Henry Clay, Chief Justice Marshall wrote:

> You are certainly right in supposing that I feel a deep interest in the character of the person who may succeed [Trimble]. His successor will, of course, be designated by Mr. Adams, because he will be required to perform the most important duties of his office, before a change in administration can take place. Mr. Crittenden is not personally known to me. . . . Were I myself to designate the successor of Mr. Trimble, I do not know the man I could prefer to him. . . .

Not everyone agreed with Chief Justice Marshall that it was President Adams' duty to choose the replacement for Trimble during the waning months of his administration. It was common knowledge that President-Elect Jackson and his advisors intended to place Jackson supporters in as many important positions as possible. Indeed, the phrase "To the Victor, Belongs the Spoils" has been credited to the Jacksonian Presidency.

On December 17, 1828, President Adams sent Crittenden's name to the Senate. It soon became evident, however, that with the majority of the Senators being supporters of President-Elect Jackson, the Senate would not act on any nominations until President Adams' term had ended and Jackson had been inaugurated as President. This decision infuriated many of Adams' supporters. One wrote to Crittenden:

> What set of corrupt scoundrels, and what an infernal precedent they are about to establish . . . Whether the spirit of party over the sense of constitutional obligation . . . will be tested by the disposition which may be made of your

nomination. We still hope that there will be a sufficient number of Jackson supporters to carry the nomination, who will rise above the disgraceful and degrading party feeling which would snatch from the present executive the power of appointment.

On December 3, 1828, Crittenden, in a letter to Henry Clay, wrote: ". . . As to the Federal judgeship to which you say I have been recommended, I have only to remark that if it should come to me, neither the giving nor the receiving of it shall be soiled by any solicitations of mine on the subject." In another letter to Clay dated January 16, 1829, he wrote: "Whatever may be the fate of my nomination in the Senate, I am prepared to bear it with fortitude and resignation, though in rejection there is a taste of dishonor which my nature revolts at."

On February 12, 1829, the Senate voted twenty-three to seventeen that it was inexpedient to act upon the nomination.

There is no doubt that Crittenden was well-qualified to become an Associate Justice of the Supreme Court of the United States. One can only speculate whether if the Jacksonian Senators had voted to confirm Crittenden, a precedent would have been set that future Supreme Court nominees would be considered solely on their qualifications and not on their politics.

Crittenden was subsequently appointed Attorney-General in the Fillmore administration, and then served in the United States Senate from 1855 to 1861.

Chapter Five

President Andrew Jackson
7th President (1829-1837)
Party affiliation: Democrat

Supreme Court nomination not confirmed
by the United States Senate:

ROGER BROOKE TANEY
Born: March 17, 1777
Died: October 12, 1864
Education: Dickinson College,
Read law in judge's office
Nominated Associate Justice,
January 15, 1835
Postponed, March 3, 1835
Nominated Chief Justice,
December 28, 1835
Confirmed by Senate,
March 15, 1836

Taney is well-known as the Chief Justice who authored the famous (or infamous) *Dred Scott* decision that many historians cite as one of the crucial causes of the Civil War. This decision probably resulted in the contrary views about his reputation. For example, shortly after his death in 1864, Judge William Giles of the United States District Court in Maryland said:

> For eleven years I have been associated in the Federal courts in this state with this great man. ... Now, when he has passed away and no word of mine can affend [sic] his modesty, I can truly say that I have never known a purer or better man, one who loved his country more, or whose heart was more alive to every warm and generous feeling of our nature.

Yet at about the same time, a "Memorial" published anonymously in New York said:

> As a man, a Christian, and a Jurist, he falls below the latest standard of humanity, religion and law recognized among civilized man. . . . As a Jurist, or more strictly speaking, as a Judge, in which

character he will be most remembered, he was next to Pontious Pilate, perhaps the worst that ever occupied the seat of judgement [sic] among men.

It is interesting to speculate on what this anonymous critic would think if he could have known that a hundred and forty years later, leading academic constitutional scholars would include Taney among the twelve all-time greatest Supreme Court Justices!

Taney (pronounced Tawney) is included in these *Sketches* as, just fifteen months before becoming Chief Justice, he was nominated as an Associate Justice and failed to receive the consent of the Senate.

Taney was originally active in Maryland politics and was elected to public office as a Federalist. But as that Party began its decline, he became an active supporter of Andrew Jackson and was appointed Attorney-General in President Jackson's Cabinet in 1831.

During Jackson's first term, the matter of the continuing existence of the Bank of the United States came before the Congress. President Jackson and the Democratic Party were vehemently against its continuance while the Whigs were just as vehemently in favor of it. In 1832 the Congress passed legislation renewing the Charter of the Bank but Jackson vetoed it. The next year President Jackson ordered the Secretary of the Treasury to withdraw money from the Bank of the United States but he refused to do so. Jackson then replaced him with an interim appointment of Taney as Secretary of the Treasury. When his name came before the Senate, however, it was rejected and Taney returned to private life in Maryland.

In 1835, a seat on the Supreme Court became vacant upon the resignation of Associate Justice Gabriel Duvall. On January 15, 1835, Jackson nominated Taney to succeed Duvall. The Whigs (successors to the Federalists) opposed this appointment and viewed it as a prize offered to Taney for his previous support of Jackson's programs. Although Taney, both by experience and education, was fully qualified to become an Associate Justice, this was overlooked by the Whigs in their effort to punish him for the loyalty he had given to President Jackson while he was a member of the Executive Branch. The *Washington Globe* on February 11, 1835, wrote:

> We hope that the Senate will not only apply the veto to the pretensions of this man, but that it will pass a decided resolution to oppose the elevation of any man who is not perfectly sound in regard to the fundamental principles of the constitution as expounded by Daniel Webster.

The *New York Courier* on January 19, 1835, commented that:

> Mr. Taney will be rejected and I should think properly rejected. . . . It is full time that public men should be made to feel that offices of honor and emolument are not solely of the Executive, and that subserviency to his will or truckling to his behest is not enough to secure to them the reward they anticipated.

There were some, however, who did recognize Taney's ability and among them was Chief Justice John Marshall who wrote a Virginia Senator that "if you have not made up your mind on the nomination of Mr. Taney, I have some information in his favor which I wish to communicate."

But partisan opposition did take preference. In 1835 the Whigs still had a majority in the Senate and delayed moving action on the nomination until the last day of the final session of the Congress when it postponed, by a vote of twenty-four to twenty-one, taking any action on Taney, effectively rejecting the appointment of Taney as an Associate Justice.

When, however, the new Congress met in December 1835, Jackson's supporters in the Senate were now in the majority. Chief Justice John Marshall had died in July 1835 and on December 28, 1835, President Jackson nominated Roger Taney as Chief Justice. He was confirmed by the Senate on March 15, 1836.

It is of interest to speculate whether the *Dred Scott* decision might have turned out differently if the Senate had confirmed Taney as an Associate Justice. It is likely if that had happened President Jackson might have appointed some one else Chief Justice upon the death of Chief Justice Marshall.

Professor Fehrenbacher, in his authoritative study, *The Dred Scott Decision, Its Significance in American Law and Politics*, discusses how the *Dred Scott* opinion was originally assigned to Justice Nelson, who produced a short draft opinion that avoided the crucial issues of whether Congress had the power to regulate slavery in the territories. He then indicates that the majority of the Justices reversed themselves and decided that this question should be covered and that Taney should write the opinion. Historians have differed on what made the majority change its mind. Fehrenbacher suggests that Taney may have had a greater role in that decision when he writes:

Yet one should not discard the possibility that Taney played a more important part than is visible on the surface. Behind his mask of judicial propriety, the Chief Justice had become a bitter sectionalist, seething with anger at the "Northern insult and aggression."

Thus, it might be considered that Taney as an Associate Justice rather than as Chief Justice would not have been as influential as he appears to have been in persuading the Court to take the position that it did on the slavery question.

Chapter Six

President John Tyler
10th President (1841-1845)
Party affiliation: Whig

Supreme Court nominations not confirmed
by the United States Senate:

JOHN C. SPENCER
Born: January 8, 1788
Died: May 17, 1855
Education: Union College, NY
Read law in law office
Nominated Associate Justice,
January 9, 1844
Rejected by Senate,
January 31, 1844

REUBEN H. WALWORTH
Born: October 26, 1788
Died: November 28, 1867
Education: Self-educated,
Read law in law office
Nominated Associate Justice,
March 13, 1844
Withdrawn, June 17, 1844

EDWARD KING
Born: January 31, 1794
Died: May 8, 1873
Education: Self-educated,
Read law in law office
Nominated Associate Justice,
June 5, 1844
Postponed, June 15, 1844
Nominated again,
December 4, 1844
Withdrawn, February 7, 1845

JOHN M. READ
Born: July 21, 1797
Died: November 29, 1874
Education: Univ of Pennsylvania
Read law in law office
Nominated Associate Justice,
February 7, 1845
No action taken by Senate

President Tyler has the dubious honor of making six nominations to the Supreme Court and having five of these rejected by the Senate, a record not equaled by any subsequent President. To understand why this happened will require a brief excursion into the political scene at the time of the 1840 election year. Martin Van Buren, who became President in 1837 following the popular Andrew Jackson, was in political trouble. This was due primarily to the economic depression that occurred shortly after Van Buren became President and lasted throughout his term. Although he was nominated by the Democratic Party for reelection in 1840, it was generally felt that he could not win this election.

When the Whigs met in convention in 1840, the two leading candidates were Henry Clay of Kentucky and Daniel Webster of Massachusetts. The Whigs were anxious to have a candidate who not only could win the election, but who would not follow what the Whigs considered to be Jackson's dictatorial and disastrous policies. When it became evident that neither Clay nor Webster could obtain a majority of the votes of the delegates, the Convention turned to William Henry Harrison. Harrison was a war hero having in 1811 led his troops against the Shawnee Indians at Tippecanoe Creek, which was considered a significant victory by white settlers. General Harrison also played an important role in the War of 1812 and subsequently was elected to the House of Representatives from Ohio and then to the United States Senate.

When Daniel Webster threw his support to Harrison, the Convention nominated him. Harrison then succeeded in defeating Van Buren in the Presidential election. But thirty-one days after his inauguration, Harrison died and John Tyler assumed the Presidency.

Tyler was selected as Vice-President without too much thought, for, as typical then as now, the emphasis was on a candidate who would balance the ticket rather than focusing on the ideology of the candidate. Norma Patterson in her book *The Presidencies of William Henry Harrison and John Tyler* commented that:

> As in most political conventions, the selection of the Vice-President was perfunctory. Not until Tyler became President and clashed head-on with Clay and other nationally minded Whigs did his detractors question how the delegates, if in full possession of their senses, have chosen John Tyler.

Conflict between Tyler and the Congressional Whigs began almost immediately after Tyler's inauguration and reached its climax a year later when the Whigs formally expelled Tyler from the Whig Party. With the Whigs now controlling the Senate by a majority of twenty-eight to twenty-three, Tyler had a great deal of conflict with the Senate, including his failure to receive its consent for five of his Supreme Court nominations.

Tyler's first opportunity to appoint a Supreme Court Justice came when Associate Justice Smith Thompson died on December 18, 1843. At that time, President Tyler was in constant disagreement with the Congressional Whigs and rumors were widespread that Tyler intended to stand for reelection in 1844 as a Democrat. Considering also that Tyler was entering the last year of his first term, it is difficult to understand why he nominated, on January 9, 1844, John C. Spencer for the vacant Supreme Court seat.

Spencer was a New York lawyer and had a distinguished career in Congress before being appointed Secretary of War by President Tyler. He was recognized as an able and scholarly lawyer and suitable to sit on the Supreme Court. But he had several counts against him that President Tyler should have realized would make his confirmation by the Senate difficult, if not impossible. By accepting an appointment in Tyler's Cabinet, Spencer had made enemies of those Whig Senators who were strong supporters of Henry Clay. He was also notoriously short-tempered and his abrupt personality caused many other Senators to dislike him. Finally, the Whigs considered him a political traitor for giving his support to Tyler. The Senate on January 31 voted twenty-six to twenty-one not to give its advice and consent.

After the Senate refused to confirm Spencer, Justice Story wrote in a letter to a friend that:

No one can conjecture what we shall have as a new Judge. . . . I have my own wishes on the subject, strong and warm, but I have no hope that they will be gratified. I want an associate of the highest integrity, with youth and ambition enough to make him become a deep student in all the law, and with a spirit of love for the Constitution and an independence to proclaim it, which shall make him superior to all popular clamors - and these to be united with courtesy of manners and kindness of heart. These, I admit, are high qualities; but I think I could find them.

President Tyler on March 13, 1844, next nominated Reuben H. Walworth of New York, a lawyer with well-known legal abilities but hardly one to meet Justice Story's qualifications. He had been appointed to the Office of Chancellor for the State of New York in 1828. (In England the courts were separated into courts of law and courts of equity, with the latter headed by a Chancellor which was the equivalent of a Chief Judge. This practice was carried over to many of the states in this country. By the beginning of the twentieth century, however, nearly every state had merged these two courts into a unified court system.)

On assuming the duties of Chancellor, Walworth made an address to the New York State Bar, where he said: ". . . Brought up as a farmer until the age of seventeen, deprived of all the advantages of a classical education, and with very limited knowledge of Chancery law, I find myself at the age of thirty-eight, suddenly and unexpectedly placed at the head of the judiciary of the State; a situation which heretofore has been filled by the most able and experienced members of the profession."

Aaron Burr allegedly wrote Walworth and advised him not to publish the address "because if the people read this they will exclaim, 'Then if you knew you were not qualified, why the devil did you take the office?'"

Walworth served for twenty years as Chancellor and made significant contributions to the jurisprudence of New York. But Walworth was disliked by the Whigs; just how much is demonstrated by remarks made in a letter by Senator Crittenden as quoted in Warren's *Supreme Court in United States History*:

He [Walworth] is recommended by many distinguished Members of the Bar of [New York] State *merely because they are anxious to get rid of a querulous, disagreeable, unpopular Chancellor.* Indeed so odious is he that our [New York] Senate, when a majority of his own political friends were members, voted to abolish the office of Chancellor.

But in an article published in *Portraits of Eminent Americans Now Living* in 1853, a different view of him is presented. For example, the author states that:

No one can examine the volumes of Chancellor Walworth's reported adjudications without being satisfied, not only that he is a profound lawyer, but that his attainments in all collateral branches of learning are most extensive; and that in no respect does he yield to any judge by whom the judicial annals of our state have been illustrated.

The Senate, however, voted on June 15 to postpone taking action on him, and on June 17 Tyler withdrew his name. In retrospect it appears that Walworth was a self-educated and self-made man who did not receive the consent of the Senate because of the timing of his appointment. If confirmed he most likely would have made a competent Justice, but not a great one.

While Walworth's nomination was awaiting confirmation by the Senate, President Tyler was faced with another vacancy on the Court caused by the death of Justice Henry Baldwin on April 21, 1844. To fill this position, Tyler, on June 5, 1844, nominated Edward King, a distinguished Pennsylvania judge and lawyer. Several factors combined to make his confirmation difficult. This was the last year of Tyler's term and it was an election year. The differences between Tyler and the Whig Senate were greater than ever. Moreover, the Whig candidate for President was Henry Clay and it was believed that if he won, Senator Crittenden, who failed confirmation during the last days of John Quincy Adams presidency, would be appointed to the Supreme Court.

Consequently, the Senate delayed action on King's nomination. Entirely unfair to King, one Whig newspaper wrote: "Better the Bench should be vacant for a year, than filled for half a century by corrupt or feeble men, or partisans committed in advance to particular beliefs." Despite, however, some strong support for King's fitness for the position, politics won out and his consideration by the Senate was postponed on June 15, 1844. Although in the November election Tyler was defeated by his Democratic opponent, James Polk, he again sent King's name to the Senate on December 4, 1844. On February 7, 1845, when it became apparent that the Senate would not confirm King, Tyler withdrew his name. On that same day he nominated John M. Read for the vacant Baldwin seat.

Read was a leader of the Philadelphia Bar and highly respected for his legal abilities and for his character. But not everyone agreed as to his qualifications, and Richard Peters, former Reporter for the Supreme Court, wrote that "[i]f King is rejected the next nominee will be John M. Read, as suited for a Judge as I am for an admiral." Actually, Read had little chance of confirmation regardless of his qualifications. It was less than a month before the end of Tyler's term of office with a Democratic President replacing him. This in addition to Read's anti-slavery position made it certain that Congress would adjourn without taking any action on Read.

Tyler did have one success with a Supreme Court nomination by withdrawing Walworth's name and submitting that of Samuel Nelson. At the time, Nelson had been a Judge on the Supreme Court of New York for fourteen years, seven of them as Chief Judge. He was fifty-two years old and recognized as a person of great ability. Nelson was confirmed on February 14, 1845, only ten days after his nomination was submitted to the Senate.

This does illustrate that if Presidents are sincerely interested in appointing the "very best qualified person," they can obtain Senate confirmation despite political affiliation or other considerations.

In summary, this is the scorecard of President Tyler's nominations to the Supreme Court:

Name	Date of Nomination	Date of Senate Action	To Replace
Spencer	1/9/44	1/31/44 Rejected	Thompson
Walworth	3/13/44	6/17/44 Withdrawn	Thompson
King	6/5/44	6/15/44 Postponed	Baldwin
King	12/4/44	2/7/45 Withdrawn	Baldwin
Nelson	2/4/45	2/14/45 Confirmed	Thompson
Read	2/7/45	No Action	Baldwin

Chapter Seven

President James K. Polk
11th President (1845-1849)
Party affiliation: Democrat

Supreme Court nomination not confirmed
by the United States Senate:

GEORGE W. WOODWARD
Born: March 26, 1809
Died: May 10, 1875
Education: Read law in law
office
Nominated Associate Justice,
November 23, 1845
Rejected by Senate,
January 22, 1846

When James Polk was elected President in 1844 there was still a vacancy on the Supreme Court, carried over from the previous administration of President Tyler.

President Polk encountered much the same difficulties as did Tyler in filling this vacancy. To understand why, it will be necessary to discuss the political career of Polk. He was from Tennessee and was elected to Congress in 1825. When Andrew Jackson, a Democrat, became President in 1832, Polk was the acknowledged leader of the Democrats in the House of Representatives, and he continued to be a loyal supporter of President Jackson. Polk became involved in a close and bitter race for Speaker of the House, and was defeated by an enemy of Jackson. Polk, however, was elected Speaker in the next Session of Congress, and remained a favorite of Jackson.

In 1844 Andrew Jackson, now a past President, remained an active leader of the Democratic Party and was supporting Van Buren for the Democratic nomination for President. But events occurred that changed his mind. President Tyler had made annexation of Texas an important political issue and the two leading candidates (Clay and Van Buren) were requested to state their views on this question. When Van Buren wrote a letter against the annexation of Texas, Jackson became convinced that Van Buren was not electable and decided to throw his support to Polk. At the 1844 Democratic Convention it was necessary for a candidate to receive the nomination by a two-thirds majority. Neither Clay nor Van Buren could obtain this, and with Jackson's support, Polk was nominated, thus becoming the first "dark horse" to receive a nomination from a political convention.

When Polk became President, the Democrats had a majority of five in the Senate but several of them were enemies of Polk and he could not always rely on their support.

There was another factor that impeded Polk's choosing a person for the Supreme Court. Before 1891, the lower federal courts consisted of the district courts and the circuit courts. By statute, each circuit consisted of two or more states and a Supreme Court Justice was assigned to a circuit and "rode the circuit" trying cases in various cities within the circuit. Early in the nineteenth century, the custom developed that when a Supreme Court seat became vacant, the President was supposed to fill it with a person from the same circuit.

For the current vacancy, this meant someone from either New Jersey or Pennsylvania. Polk's Secretary of State was James Buchanan, a former Pennsylvania Senator. Another possibility was Simon Cameron, a present Senator from Pennsylvania but a long-time foe of both Polk and Buchanan. President Polk noted in his diary how Buchanan was most anxious for Polk to appoint John M. Read of Philadelphia. (Read had been nominated for the vacant seat by President Tyler but the Senate adjourned without taking any action on him.)

Polk's reasons for not nominating Read are set forth in his diary:

Mr. Read, I learned, was until ten or twelve years ago a leading federalist, and a Representative of that party in the legislature. . . . I have never known an instance of a Federalist who had after arriving at the age of thirty professed a change of his opinions, who was to be relied on in his constitutional opinions. All of them who had been appointed to the Supreme court bench after securing a place for life became very soon broadly Federal and latitudinarian in all of their decisions involving questions of constitutional power. General Jackson had been most unfortunate in his appointments to that bench in this respect. I resolved to appoint no man who was not an original Democrat and strict constructionist, and who would be less likely to relapse into the broad Federal doctrines of Judge Marshall and Judge Story.

Undoubtedly, most presidents had or will have similar criteria conforming to their own political philosophy.

After Polk told Buchanan that he would not consider Read, an advisor to Polk informed him that Buchanan himself was anxious to become a Supreme Court justice. Polk then discussed the matter with Buchanan on September 19, 1845, and they agreed that Polk would nominate Buchanan, but the announcement would be withheld until Buchanan finished some pending diplomatic business. By the middle of November, however, Buchanan changed his mind and informed the President that he had decided to continue as Secretary of State.

President Polk was then advised to appoint George W. Woodward, the presiding Judge of the Fourth Judicial District of Pennsylvania and a highly respected jurist. Polk made the nomination even though he was aware of the dislike Senator

Cameron had for Judge Woodward. This was the result of a bitter senatorial election between Cameron and Woodward, with the former being successful.

But Woodward had considerable opposition from another source. This came from the reputation Woodward had as "Nativist." The 1840's had seen a tremendous influx of immigrants, mostly from Ireland and Germany, and primarily Catholic. The majority of these had settled in the northern states, and there rose in opposition an anti-immigrant movement known as the "Nativists." Earlier in Woodward's career he had made anti-immigrant speeches. His nomination therefore resulted in considerable opposition. The extent and flavor of it can best be demonstrated by examining contemporary accounts.

New York Herald (January 6, 1846):
The President at last has discovered himself to be in a rather bad box on account of Woodward's nomination for the Judgeship. He is mortified to the quick that he should have made a mistake, and given offense to so large a number of his best friends and supporters. The White House and the Senate within the last two days, have been literally overrun with protests from Philadelphia, New York, Baltimore. . . . The most respectable and influential of the Irish adopted citizens say they do not know who to trust with their interests after this. . . . The Germans, French and others shrug their shoulders and exclaim, "Mon Dieu, Mon Dieu! Monsieur Polk is one very native American."

New York Herald (January 9, 1846):
Woodward's nomination . . . will be defeated. There is already a powerful opposition organized

against him in the Senate. The whigs, committed as they are against "nativism," dare not support him, and the democrats, fearing to vote against the President's nomination on the one hand, and of offending a numerous and influential portion of the party on the other, are in such a dilemma that they know not precisely how to act.

New York Herald (January 15, 1846):
A great fuss is being made about the nomination of Judge Woodward. . . . The fuss arises because it seems that he once declared his opinion that natives of foreign countries ought not to be allowed to vote when they come to the United States. . . . If Judge Woodward has always been an intelligent and upright man, that is sufficient. We don't see how he could be prevented from holding any special opinion on politics or religion. If he is a man of integrity, and competent to decide all questions that may become before him according to the law of the land, that is all that is requisite. The fuss against him is like a tempest in a teapot.

New York Herald (January 26, 1846):
. . . I have learned that today the Senate rejected Mr. Woodward's nomination as Associate Justice of the Supreme Court. This ought to serve as a lesson to the "natives" never again to desecrate the Constitution or disgrace the character and honor of their country, by intolerance. . . . The American, of what ever party, will never countenance or support a principle so abhorrent to the finest feelings of our nature, and bring themselves, and our country down to a level with European monarchies in their system

of exclusive ruling for a benefit of a select few. The Constitution of the United States is that which makes the native as adopted as American freeman, not the accident of birth; for if this were so, "natives" so called, have done injustice to . . . their Indian brethren, in not securing for them the privileges they so zealously contend for themselves.

On January 22, 1846, the Senate rejected Woodward by a vote of twenty-nine to twenty, with all of the Whigs and six Democrats voting against Woodward.

Interestingly, despite all the expressed opposition to Woodward because of his "Nativist" sentiments, none of this is reflected by Polk in his diary. Rather, he placed the blame on a conspiracy between Buchanan and Senator Cameron, along with the dissenting Democratic Senators who were "calculated to weaken my administration, and destroy or impair my power and influence in carrying out the measures of my administration." (*Diary of President Polk,* February 11, 1846)

By July 1846, Polk and Buchanan had reconciled their differences and Buchanan let Polk know of his desire to be on the Supreme Court. They again agreed that Polk would make the appointment, but would wait until the end of the present session of Congress. But by August 1846, Buchanan once again changed his mind and decided to remain as Secretary of State.

President Polk then appointed Robert C. Grier of Pennsylvania, who was confirmed by the Senate on August 4, 1846. Thus, twenty-eight months after the death of Justice Baldwin, his seat was finally filled!

Judge Woodward was appointed in 1852 to be a Justice of

the Supreme Court of Pennsylvania where he served honorably for fifteen years.

Chapter Eight

President Millard Fillmore
13th President (1850-1853)
Party affiliation: Whig

Supreme Court nominations not confirmed
by the United States Senate:

EDWARD A. BRADFORD
Born: September 27, 1813
Died: November 22, 1872
Education: Delaware College,
Read law in law office
Nominated Associate Justice,
August 16, 1852
No action taken by Senate

GEORGE E. BADGER
Born: April 17, 1795
Died: May 11, 1866
Education: Yale University (2 years),
Read law in law office
Nominated Associate Justice,
January 10, 1853
Senate postponed action,
February 11, 1853

WILLIAM C. MICOU
Born: 1806
Died: April 16, 1854
Education: Read law in '
law office
Nominated Associate Justice,
February 24, 1853
No action taken by Senate

53

During 1848 it became evident that President Polk was determined to fulfill his promise not to be a candidate for a second term. Moreover, many events during Polk's Administration, such as the Mexican War, the increasing antagonism between the North and South over the slavery issue, as well as other political matters of the time made it predictable that the Whigs would gain the White House in the forthcoming 1848 election.

The Whigs once again nominated a war hero with little governmental experience. The one they chose was Zachary Taylor, the hero of the Mexican War and known as "Old Rough and Ready."

For Vice-President, the Whigs sought a Northerner who could balance the ticket against the slave-holder and Southerner Zachary Taylor. They chose Millard Fillmore, a former Governor of New York and well known in the North. Fate intervened, however, and President Taylor died on July 9, 1850, only sixteen months after his inauguration. Thus, nine years after the death of President Harrison, the country once again saw the term of the elected President cut short and the Vice-President assuming the Office of President.

Fillmore's first opportunity to appoint a Supreme Court Justice came in September, 1851, with the death of Justice Levi Woodbury. Fillmore nominated Benjamin R. Curtis, a prominent scholar and Boston attorney, and the Senate confirmed him shortly thereafter. An interesting insight into Curtis's beliefs became apparent when in 1857 he wrote a strong dissenting opinion in the *Dred Scott* decision and shortly thereafter resigned in protest from the Court.

Another seat on the Court became vacant upon the death of Justice John McKinley on July 10, 1852. Fillmore made three nominations but was unable to obtain Senate confirmation for any of them, as the vacancy occurred during the last year of his term and the Democrats were anticipating victory in the forthcoming election.

On August 16, 1852, President Fillmore nominated Edward A. Bradford, a prominent Louisiana lawyer, to become an Associate Supreme Court Justice. Congress, however, adjourned shortly thereafter without taking any action on the nomination of Bradford.

The election for President took place in November of that year. The Whigs refused to nominate Fillmore for a second term and instead nominated Winfield Scott, a former General and hero of the Mexican War.

The Democrats, after forty-nine ballots, nominated Franklin Pierce of New Hampshire, a Jacksonian Democrat who had served as a Brigadier General under Winfred Scott. Due to the split of the Whigs into Northern Whigs and Southern Whigs, Franklin Pierce was elected President. Fillmore, however, would remain in Office until March 1853, and he was determined to exercise his constitutional right to nominate a Supreme Court candidate. He selected George E. Badger, a Senator from North Carolina who had served as Secretary of the Navy under Presidents Harrison and Tyler. Although he was not from the same circuit as the Justice he would replace, it seemed to be a wise choice as he was considered neither pro-slavery nor anti-slavery. It was thought that the Senate would exercise Senatorial courtesy and not reject a fellow Senator.

On January 8, 1853, the *New York Daily Tribune* ran a peculiar story on Badger.

> This iron-heeled Old Fogy is nominated for the Supreme Bench . . . and we hope his nomination will be confirmed. He is a lawyer of unsurpassing abilities, and in the main, we believe an upright man. . . . Yet Mr. Badger [is] by no means a great man. But it is by no means necessary to be a great man in order to be a great lawyer. Mr. Badger's qualifications for the place to which he is nominated, are a tough,´ hard, wiry, mental organization . . . with a good knowledge of the law.

> As a statesman he is of no account, and as a politician detestable. He lacks breadth and comprehensiveness of view. . . . His mind ran in the rut of the law so long before he came into public life that he always gets out of gearing whenever he is wanted for a pull out of the beaten track. . . . He has not a single agreeable or winning qualification as a public man. Wrong-headed, crabbed, intolerant, dogmatical, inveterate in his prejudices, dictatorial and unmannerly in his deportment, we have often wondered how he ever

got into his present position. . . . He is reserved, aristocratic and exclusive, exhibiting an offensive prominence of the idea of *caste*, which is often ludicrously in the decayed, shabby gentility of old Virginia gentlemen.

Yet not withstanding all this we don't think Mr. Badger would make a bad Judge.

One must wonder what this reporter would write about a judicial candidate he did not like!

But the Senate consisted of thirty-six Democrats and only twenty Whigs, and on February 11, 1853, they postponed taking any action on Badger until March 4, when the new President would be inaugurated, with the right to choose his own nominee. The *New York Times*, after the Senate had postponed taking any action on Badger's nomination, carried the following story.

The rejection by the United States Senate of Mr. Badger's nomination for Judge of the Supreme Court, is one of those purely party operations which the country will not sustain. There was no possible objection to the Senator from North Carolina, except that he is a Whig. No man dared utter a word against his private character; no breath of suspicion has tarnished his fame as a jurist; and there are none to be found to dispute that he would have carried to the position to which the President desired his elevation, distinguished abilities, great caution, brilliant intellect, profound attainments, and the most scrupulous regard for the blind goddess whose decrees it would have become his duty to dispense. But the deed is done. All considerations of justice and the public good have been sacrificed to partisan zeal, and the country will hold to their responsibility the Senators who have so abused the trust confided to them.

President Fillmore made another attempt to fill the vacant seat, but this time he was determined to choose a lawyer from the same circuit (Alabama and Louisiana). He offered to nominate Judah P. Benjamin, a prominent Louisiana lawyer recently elected to the United States Senate. But Benjamin declined, preferring to remain in the Senate. His subsequent history is of interest. In 1861 when Louisiana seceded from the Union, Benjamin resigned from the United States Senate and Jefferson Davis appointed him Attorney-General in the Confederate Cabinet. He subsequently held the positions of Secretary of War and Secretary of State in the Confederate Government. After General Lee surrendered to General Grant, Benjamin managed to escape to England where he became a well-known Barrister and author of the popular *Benjamin on Sales*.

After Benjamin declined the nomination, on February 24, 1853, Fillmore nominated William C. Micou, a law partner of Benjamin. It was, however, too close to the end of Fillmore's term and the Democratic Senate refused to take any action. The vacant seat remained for the incoming President Pierce to fill.

Chapter Nine

President James Buchanan
15th President (1857-1861)
Party affiliation: Democrat

Supreme Court nomination not confirmed
by the United States Senate:

JEREMIAH S. BLACK
Born: January 10, 1810
Died: August 19, 1883
Education: Self-educated,
Read law in law office
Nominated Associate Justice,
February 5, 1861
Rejected by Senate,
February 21, 1861

The election of 1856 was a crucial one for the United States. The Democrats had nominated James Buchanan of Pennsylvania, the Republicans, John C. Fremont of California, and a third party, the American Know Nothing, nominated Millard Fillmore. The most controversial issue in the election was the question of slavery in the Territories; public opinion on this question was divided between the North and the South. Buchanan received the majority of the Electoral College vote but not the majority of the popular votes due to the presence of the third party on the ballot.

When Buchanan was inaugurated in March 1857, the Supreme Court had, in addition to Chief Justice Taney, five pro-slavery justices from the South and four anti-slavery justices from the North. It remained so until Associate Justice Peter V. Daniel died on May 30, 1860, leaving the court split between four justices from the South and four from the North. As Justice Daniel had been from Virginia, Southerners strongly urged the President to appoint another Justice from the South because, "The appointment of a successor to Daniel is of little less importance to the South than the election of the next President." The Northern Republicans, however, were just as insistent that no further representative of the slavery interest should be appointed.

63

Buchanan had decided to nominate Jeremiah S. Black of Pennsylvania. Black had been a trial judge and later was elected to the Pennsylvania Supreme Court. He had been active in the Democratic Party and had been a long-time supporter of Buchanan. He held similar opinions with the President in opposition to slavery but with strong beliefs in state rights. Both Buchanan and Black felt that the Federal government was powerless to interfere with slavery in the Southern states. In 1857 the President had appointed Black as Attorney-General, where he subsequently issued an opinion stating that the President can not coerce a seceding state to remain and that the only authority the President has under the Constitution is to protect Federal property.

When the Secretary of State resigned in 1860, Buchanan appointed Black to that position.

Although the Supreme Court seat had become vacant on May 30, 1860, President Buchanan did not nominate Black until February 5, 1861. By this time, the Presidential election of 1860 had taken place resulting in the election of the Republican candidate, Abraham Lincoln, and his inauguration was less than a month away.

At the time, there was considerable discussion and doubt as to why Buchanan had delayed making the appointment. It later became known that he had expected the resignation of Chief Justice Taney who was nearly 84 and in ill health. But Taney did not resign and the President finally made the nomination of Jeremiah Black on February 5, 1861.

It was, however, too late. The inauguration of Lincoln was only a few weeks away. Twelve southern senators had resigned from the Senate as the states they represented had seceded from the Union. Consequently, by a close vote of twenty-five in favor and twenty-six against, the Senate refused to confirm Black's nomination.

In 1869 Black was in a serious accident which deprived him of the use of his right arm. However he continued to play an active role in the political and social life of the nation. In 1886 a relative, Chauncey F. Black, published a volume of Jeremiah's essays and speeches that demonstrated his extensive knowledge of many different subjects. Of particular interest is a speech he gave on September 17, 1856, at Pennsylvania College. In it he expounded that:

> The manifest object of the men who framed the institutions of this country, was to have a *State without religion*, and a *Church without politics* -- that is to say, they meant that one should never be used as an engine for any purpose of the other, and that no man's rights in one should be tested by his opinions about the other. As the Church takes no note of a man's political differences, so the State looks with equal eye on all the modes of religious faith. The Church may give her preferment to a Tory, and the State may be served by a heretic. Our Fathers seem to have been perfectly sincere in their belief that the members of the Church would be more patriotic, and the citizens of the state more religious, by keeping their separate functions entirely separate. For that reason they built up a wall of complete and perfect partion between the two.

It is interesting to notice that ninety-one years later, his namesake Associate Justice Hugo Black used similar language in a landmark case on religion and the state in Everson v. Board of Education, 330 U. S. 1 at 15 (1947).

Chapter Ten

President Andrew Johnson
17th President (1865-1869)
Party affiliation: Democrat

Supreme Court nomination not confirmed
by the United States Senate

HENRY STANBERY
Born: February 20, 1803
Died: June 26, 1881
Education: Washington College, Pa.
Read law in law office
Nominated Associate Justice,
    April 16, 1866
    No action taken by Senate

President Lincoln was assassinated on April 14, 1865, and Andrew Johnson became the third Vice-President within twenty-four years to be elevated to the Presidency. He was in a similar position as the previous two Vice-Presidents (James Tyler and Millard Fillmore) in that he had been chosen to balance the ticket, rather than on his own merits, and he faced a Congress opposed to many of his policies. It indeed was much more difficult for Johnson as the Civil War had recently ended and the Congress was controlled by the Radical Republicans who were determined to enact Reconstruction legislation much stricter than either Lincoln or Johnson had envisioned.

When a Supreme Court seat became vacant in May 1865 due to the death of Associate Justice John Catron, the Court consisted of the Chief Justice and nine Associate Justices. The first Supreme Court had consisted of six justices; by 1837 the number of justices had been raised to nine. In 1863, Congress added an additional seat to compensate for the new circuit consisting of California and Oregon. Supreme Court Justices were still required to travel to their assigned circuit when not in session in Washington.

President Johnson waited almost a year before making an

appointment. He nominated Henry Stanbery to become an Associate Justice on April 16, 1866. Stanbery was born in New York City in 1803, but his family moved soon thereafter to Ohio. He was admitted to the Ohio Bar when he was twenty-one. In 1846 he became the Ohio Attorney-General and then practiced law in Cincinnati until appointed United States Attorney-General by President Johnson. Gideon Welles, who was Secretary of Navy in Johnson's Cabinet, noted in his *Diary* on April 17, 1866:

> In nominating Stanbery to the Supreme Court, he [the President] had a desire to get a sound man on the bench, one who was right on fundamental constitutional questions. Stanbery, he says, is with us thoroughly, earnestly.

Similarly, *The Nation* on April 26, 1866, described Stanbery as ". . . a man of the highest character, and a lawyer of very unusual ability." The *Philadelphia Enquirer* on April 18, 1866, wrote:

> The Hon. Henry G. Stanbery, of Cincinnati who was nominated on Monday for the vacancy on the Supreme Court . . . is a most excellent appointment, and it is to be hoped that he will be promptly confirmed by the Senate. . . . He was originally an old Whig, and voted for Buchanan. But in 1860, being a personal friend of Mr. Lincoln, he voted for him, and has since been for sustaining the war. Lately he has been in close and intimate relations with the President. He is about sixty years of age, and is of the highest professional integrity. Mr. Stanbery's power of legal analysis, close reasoning, accuracy of statement and concise and forcible expression,

have justly placed him at the head of the present
Bar of the Supreme Court. Being a man of great
industry, his accession to the Bench will be most
satisfactory to the other members of the Court.

As it turned out, however, Stanbery's qualifications made
little difference, for it is doubtful if any appointment by President
Johnson could have received confirmation by a Senate controlled
by the Radical Republicans. Two factors would make it
particularly difficult for Stanbery. In 1866, the Supreme Court
in its decision in *Ex Parte Milligan* held that one could not be
tried in military courts in areas where civil courts were in
operation. This infuriated the Radical Republicans who felt that
by this decision all their plans for reconstruction would be
endangered. The Republicans would only confirm a Supreme
Court nominee who they were confident would vote to overturn
this decision.

Another factor mitigating against Stanbery was his role
while Attorney-General in encouraging President Johnson in
vetoing a Civil Rights law that the Republican Senators highly
favored. One historian of the Court in his book (H. Abraham,
Justices and Presidents) surmised that "[i]t is doubtful that the
Senate would have approved God himself had he been nominated
by Andrew Johnson."

The Nation, in an article that called Stanbery extremely
qualified, went on to state that it had

. . . on general principles the strongest objection
to seeing enquiries instituted into a man's political
views for the purposes of ascertaining his fitness
for a seat on the judicial bench . . . the truth is
that the Supreme Court does not simply declare

the law; it to a certain extent shapes the polity of the country, and the opinions of its judges as to the fundamental structures of the Government are, and will be for some time to come, of the last importance.

As matters developed, however, the Senate did not have to make the decision on whether or not to confirm Stanbery. On February 26, 1866, before the President submitted Stanbery's name, a bill was introduced into the House of Representatives to reduce the number of Supreme Court justices to nine. After the House passed the bill and while it was under consideration by the Senate, it was amended to further reduce the number of Supreme Court seats to seven. With this amended language, the bill became a law. Thus there was no vacancy for Stanbery to fill.

It is not clear from the legislative history of this law what was the true intent of Congress. Probably the original language of reducing the number of justices to nine reflected a valid opinion of many members of Congress that ten was an unwieldy number for the Court. The Senate's action in reducing the number to seven undoubtedly was taken to prevent President Johnson from appointing any more justices. This can be seen by the following dialogue from the *Congressional Globe* of July 18, 1866, while the Senate had this proposed change under consideration.

Mr. Wentworth. I ask the gentleman from Iowa if this bill abolishes the judge whose appointment the President sent to the Senate the other day.

Mr. Wilson of Iowa. This is a bill which passed the House before any nomination was made.

Mr. Wentworth. Does it abolish the new judgeship?

Mr. Wilson of Iowa. It abolishes the new judgeship, and provides for the reduction of the number of judges, as vacancies may occur, to six. I know that a number of the members of the Supreme Court think it will be a vast improvement.

Actually, the law provided for seven justices:

> That no vacancy in the office of associate justice of the supreme court shall be filled by appointment until the number of associate justices shall be reduced to six; and thereafter the said supreme court shall consist of a chief justice of the United States and six associate justices.... (14 U.S. Statutes-at-Large 209)

After the law became effective abolishing the seat for which Stanbery had been nominated, President Johnson nominated Stanbery to become Attorney-General again, and this was confirmed by the Senate. But early in 1868 the House of Representatives instituted and passed impeachment proceedings against Andrew Johnson. Stanbery then resigned as Attorney-General in order to become chief defense counsel for Johnson during his impeachment trial by the Senate. By one vote the Senate refused to impeach Johnson.

An accurate assessment of what Stanbery could have contributed to the Court as an Associate Justice can be ascertained from an article published after his death in the 1886-87 issue of the *Albany Law Journal*.

The fact is, that Mr. Stanbery had very great literary ability, and his study of the classics, ancient and modern, gave him a style as rich as it was simple and direct. . . . He loved the law, and brought into the practice of it the natural dignity and reverence which formerly prevailed between the Roman patron and his client. It was an old saying that "all roads lead to Rome," and with Mr. Stanbery, all branches of learning and science were useful and necessary to the advocate; as in the manifold diversity of suits, there is no line of study or thought -- music, chemistry, physiology, anatomy, mathematics, poetry, painting -- but would some time or other, be called upon in the legal forum to aid in judicial examination and judgment. . . . His elevation to the bench would have been the natural and fitting tribute to his pre-eminence merits and worth.

A more modern appraisal has been made by Henry Abraham in his book *Justices and Presidents* where he states: ". . . one of the ablest men rejected for the Supreme Court was Henry Stanbery."

Chapter Eleven

President Ulysses S. Grant
18th President (1869-1877)
Party affiliation: Republican

Supreme Court nominations not confirmed
by the United States Senate:

EBENEZER R. HOAR
Born: February 21, 1816
Died: January 31, 1895
Education: B.A.,LL.B.,
  Harvard University
Nominated Associate Justice,
  December 15, 1869
Rejected by Senate,
  February 3, 1870

GEORGE H. WILLIAMS
Born: March 26, 1820
Died: April 4, 1910
Education: Read law
  in law office
Nominated Chief Justice,
  December 1, 1873
Withdrawn, January 8, 1874

CALEB CUSHING
Born: January 17, 1800
Died: January 2, 1879
Education: Harvard College,
  Read law in law office
Nominated Chief Justice,
  January 9, 1874
Withdrawn, January 13, 1874

> The Grant administration may well be termed The
> Shabby Era in American Political History . . .
> Corruption was brazen and the first obedience of the
> Congress was to the rising forces of Capitalism.
> With the expose of the worst of the scandals . . . the
> lowest depth of American public morality was
> reached. These factors cannot be ignored in
> studying the politics of the Grant appointments.

This statement by Professor John P. Frank in the 1941
Wisconsin Law Review is perhaps the most succinct analysis of
the Grant administration. Not since the Tyler administration had
a President had such difficulties with his appointments of
Supreme Court Justices. In President Grant's eight years in
office, he had to nominate eight men to fill four vacancies!

The first vacancy occurred in 1869 during his first year as
President. This vacancy arose when Congress once again
decided to increase the number of Supreme Court justices to
nine. This immediately created a new seat to be filled and on
December 15, 1869, the President sent the name of Ebenezer R.
Hoar to the Senate.

On December 2, 1869, almost two weeks before Hoar was nominated, *The Nation* had an editorial on the Supreme Court that is relevant to the subsequent difficulties in the appointment of Supreme Court justices during President Grant's two terms. In the editorial it was pointed out how the "Supreme Court, from having been the most honored, became in a few short years the most despised of American institutions." It went on to comment how during the Civil War the Court had sunk lower than ever in public opinion. The battles over the Court during the Reconstruction Acts at one time threatened the Court's very existence. But, it continued, it was now necessary to restore order and to bring back harmony and justice, and it is evident that this could best be done by the judiciary. The editorial ended by noting:

> It is gratifying proof of the increased respect which the Supreme Court is held that we do not hear of any attempt to foist upon it . . . a partisan judge.

Unfortunately, this optimistic view did not last long.

Ebenezer R. Hoar was born on February 21, 1816, in Concord, Massachusetts. He was a graduate of both Harvard College and the Harvard Law School. After practicing law and serving in the Massachusetts Senate as an anti-slavery Whig, he became a lower court judge. In 1859 he became an Associate Justice of the Massachusetts Supreme Judicial Court, where he served until President Grant appointed him Attorney-General in 1868. A year later, Grant nominated him to become an Associate Justice of the Supreme Court. It was generally agreed that this was a fine appointment. *Harper's Weekly* for January 1, 1870, wrote that it was the very best that could have been made. It went on to comment that:

When Mr. Hoar was called into the Cabinet he was known in New England as one of the most able and upright of judges. He was universally respected in his state as one of the strongest men of his party; and not the least of his excellent qualities was his vigorous independence . . . and his legal learning, have undoubtedly warmly commended him to the President.

Similar sentiments were expressed in both the December 2, 1869, issue of *The Nation* and the *New York Times* of December 16, 1869, and in other newspapers. But it soon became apparent that Grant miscalculated the ill-feelings that many of the Senators had against Hoar. *Harper's Weekly,* after commenting so favorably on him, noted that there were reports from Washington that "the Judiciary Committee of the Senate will report Mr. Hoar's name without a recommendation." It went on to state:

The real ground of objection therefore, must be his hearty contempt of the system that makes the whole civil service party plunder. He has adopted perhaps the principle laid down by the President in his Message, of sustaining efficient officers "against remonstrances wholly political."

And indeed it was for mostly political reasons that a majority of Senators opposed the confirmation of Hoar. In Hoar's biography by Story and Emerson, they quote a letter written by Hoar to his wife where he says:

I am not having a very agreeable time just at present; the Senate does not act on my nomination, and there is said to be some prospect that they will not confirm it.

There were two primary reasons for the dislike of Hoar by the Senate. The first was his personality; unlike many politicians, he spoke his mind. His biographers quote a member who was in the Cabinet with Hoar who said:

When dealing with injustice or dishonesty, the edge of his humorous sarcasm cut like a knife, and the doer of the wrong had no refuge from self-contempt but in wrath and in hatred. . . .

Unfortunately for Hoar, there was plenty of dishonesty in the Grant administration.

The second and connected reason can be found in the actions of Hoar in his role as Attorney-General. Congress in the same Act that increased the number of Supreme Court Justices to nine, also created nine new Circuit Court seats. Nearly every Senator had a candidate for one of these seats, but Hoar was determined to recommend to the President only men who would "honor the bench in the performance of those judicial duties, subordinate only to those of the Supreme Court." Most of those recommended by the various Senators did not meet these standards. Thus the friction between Hoar and the Senate increased and Hoar became intolerable to those Senators who had friends to reward. Additionally, Hoar's plain manner of speaking and his sincerity did not help with the mood then existing in Washington.

In December 1869, Associate Justice Robert C. Grier, now seventy-four years old and having been on the Court since 1846, announced his resignation as of the end of January 1870. President Grant, now aware of the difficulty Hoar was facing with the Senate Judiciary Committee, thought he could appease the anti-Hoar Senators by nominating the fifty-four-year-old

Edwin M. Stanton. He was a favorite of most of the Republican Senators due to his consistent opposition to Andrew Johnson while he was in the Senate and the fact that he was also one of the Senators who voted for Johnson's impeachment. He also had a good reputation as a lawyer and had been the Attorney-General during the administration of President Buchanan. The *New York Times* on December 21, 1869, wrote: "The nomination was received on all hands . . . with the heartiest expressions of satisfaction, and the President was warmly commended for so promptly recognizing the feeling that had been made manifest in favor of this appointment." Thus, five days after his name was sent to the Senate, he was confirmed on December 20, 1869. A rather macabre event then occurred, as four days after his confirmation Stanton died from a heart attack. As Justice Grier was still a member of the Court, there was the strange situation where a sitting Justice attended the funeral of his successor!

It is interesting to compare the different evaluations of Stanton between the *New York Times*, a Republican newspaper that was very much in favor of him, and the *New York World*, a Democratic paper that had a different view. A day before Stanton died it ran a story which, among other things, called Stanton a "bloated blackguard," a "brutal Minister and a recreant lawyer," "a bully, a liar, a slanderer, a shedder of innocent blood." Twentieth-century newspapers indeed by comparison seem quite moderate.

President Grant's hope that the Stanton nomination would cause the Senate to confirm Hoar was in vain and on February 3, 1870, the Senate by a vote of twenty-four to thirty-three rejected his nomination. According to Hoar's biographers, one Senator remarking on the rejection was reported to have said, "What could you expect for a man who had snubbed seventy senators?"

President Grant finally was able to fill the two vacant Supreme Court seats. In February 1870 to replace Justice Grier he chose William Strong of Pennsylvania; for the new seat created by Congress he chose Joseph P. Bradley of New Jersey. Both had excellent and well-known legal qualifications, and neither had any political obligations or ambition. Both were quickly confirmed by the Senate. No further vacancies occurred until 1872.

The next vacancy came when Justice Samuel Nelson resigned after nearly twenty-seven years on the Court. (Nelson was the only nominee of President Tyler to be confirmed by the Senate.) President Grant was successful with his next nominee, Ward Hunt. He was one of the original founders of the Republican Party in 1856 and had both legislative and judicial experience in New York. Appointed on December 3, 1872, he was confirmed by the Senate on December 11, 1872.

On May 7, 1873, Chief Justice Salmon Chase died, giving President Grant the opportunity to make another appointment. He waited six months before so doing. The probable cause for this delay was his effort to persuade some prominent lawyers to accept the appointment of Chief Justice, but all refused for personal reasons.

There was a Cabinet meeting on December 1 and, according to the diary of Hamilton Fish, Secretary of State, the President brought up the question of the Chief Justiceship. Grant suggested Caleb Cushing, but the feeling was expressed that at the age of seventy-four he was too old to be considered. Grant then decided to nominate his Attorney-General, George H. Williams.

Williams was born on March 26, 1820, in New York State.

After reading law in a lawyer's office, he was admitted to the New York Bar in 1844. He subsequently moved to Iowa where he served as district judge from 1847 to 1852. In 1853, President Pierce appointed him Chief Justice of the Territory of Oregon where he served until 1857. After Oregon obtained statehood, he was elected in 1864 as a Republican to the United States Senate, but was defeated for reelection in 1871 and was then appointed United States Attorney-General.

At first, this nomination was received favorably. For example, the *New York Times* on December 1, 1873, wrote that his ". . . abilities are unquestioned, and whose character is above approach." *Harper's Weekly* called Williams "a man of such vigorous mind and strong will, so well grounded as a lawyer [and] . . . informed of the practice of the Supreme Court." But several days later contrary opinions began to appear in newspapers. One Democratic paper expressed the opinion that "Mr. Williams would make about as capable a Chief Justice as General Grant is a President. This is the highest compliment any intelligent man can possibly pay him."

Actually several factors converged to place difficulties in obtaining approval of Williams' appointment by the Senate. One was the feeling that his judicial and other experiences were gained primarily in the scantily populated Territory and State of Oregon and did not qualify him for the position of Chief Justice of the United States. For example, the *Albany Law Journal* wrote that:

> We have taken pains to examine the three volumes of [Iowa's] *Green[e] Reports* and find that nearly fifty per cent of his decisions while on the district bench were reversed by the [Iowa] Supreme Court. His opinions as Chief Justice of Oregon . . . are,

with scarcely an exception, on questions of trifling importance.

On Thursday, December 11, the Senate voted to adjourn to the following Monday. In the meantime, various allegations were being made against Williams. These included charges that while Attorney-General he used his office to influence decisions profiting private companies in which he held interests, and also of commingling his private funds with government funds. Another charge was that he used federal funds to purchase for his and his wife's use an expensive carriage and horses. What he purchased was a landaulet which is a carriage with a top divided into two sections that can be removed and with a raised seat outside to be used by the driver. This, of course, gave those in opposition to his appointment the opportunity to express their horror at one who "indulges in such oriental splendor" and the newspapers began calling him "Landaulet Williams." There were also rumors about his wife. In Professor Fairman's biography of Justice Samuel F. Miller, he reprints a note that Justice Miller wrote to another Associate Justice in which he commented:

> . . . Williams nomination is received with universal disgust. It is attributed to the personal influence of his wife, and remarks are made publicly as to the nature of that influence, which are of the most discreditable or rather disgraceful character.

On January 1, 1874, the *New York Tribune* wrote: "Williams may be perfectly honest, but in the opinion of ninety-one-hundredths of the members of the bar, and indeed of all men in the country qualified to judge, he is not fitted by nature, education, or training, for the position." By early January, it became clear that those opposed to Williams were using these allegations of misconduct to bolster their opposition to his appointment. The *New York Herald* on January 4 reprinted a story from the *New York Evening Post* (a Republican paper) by William Cullen Bryant who noted that both Republican journals and newspapers were opposed to the nomination. He indicated that:

> The ground of the opposition to Mr. Williams is not contained in what are popularly called the "charges" against him, which, whether true or false, do not touch the real issue in this case. Whether he was engaged as it is alleged, in shameless political intrigues in Oregon, or whether he has used the money of the State in providing a carriage for the needs of his family, are not the points in question. Supposing these allegations to be true, they of course constitute a fatal objection. . . . But, supposing them not to be true, their untruth would not be a reason for confirming the nomination. What the country feels in regard to Mr. Williams is his professional unfitness for the post to which he is named. . . . We have almost ceased to consider it [the Supreme Court] as the solemn areopagus of the nation, in which the proudest wisdom and learning sit enthroned by the side of the purest patriotism and virtue. But the trust it lost might easily be recovered and restored by a good selection for the Chief Justiceship. . . . It is no disrespect to the President on the part of the Senate to express a disapproval of his choice. . . . Their duty, indeed, to the President, as well as to the country, demands the most independent consideration of the subject. It would be an almost irretrievable error to place an inferior person for his lifetime -- which may be for the next 20 or 30 years -- in a position to review and

decide the most vital judicial questions, and that often involve the most important points of philosophy if not practical politics; and no party or personal objects should be allowed to control the judgment of the Senate.

He went on to comment that even President Washington ". . . was not exempt from constitutional surveillance of the Senate."

The *New York Tribune* on January 2, 1874, urged the Senate not to confirm Williams solely on the basis of vindicating him on account of the unproven allegations against him. It further stated that President Grant was probably the only person in public life who would think of appointing Mr. Williams as Chief Justice.

All these factors plus his realization that his many years in politics had made enemies of several Senators convinced Williams to withdraw his name. On January 7, he wrote to President Grant requesting his name be withdrawn for the position of Chief Justice.

Interestingly, twenty-five years later Mr. Williams wrote an article in a *Yale Law Journal* entitled "Reminiscences of the United States Supreme Court." In it, while commenting on his nomination, he indicates that after Chief Justice Chase died, Grant first nominated Caleb Cushing and after the Senate refused to confirm him, Grant then nominated Williams. Actually, it was just the reverse with Grant first nominating Williams and then Cushing. He further wrote that he had expected the Democratic Senators to vote against him, "but I was surprised, and so was the President, at the opposition of some of the Republican Senators. . . . I shall not go into the matter at this time; suffice to say that the reasons for the Republican opposition to me in the

Senate were not such as were given to the public by the newspapers."

With Williams' name withdrawn, Grant again faced the necessity of nominating another person for Chief Justice. As he did before choosing Williams, he once again was urged to consider promoting either Associate Justices Miller or Bradley, each of whom was anxious to become Chief Justice. But for reasons for which there is no documentary evidence, he refused to consider them. Perhaps one reason was that he recalled the explanation that Thomas Jefferson gave for George Washington refusing to choose a sitting Associate Justice to replace Chief Justice John Jay when he wrote that Washington was intending "to establish a precedent against descent of that office (Chief Justice) by seniority and to keep five (now eight) mouths always gaping for one sugar plum."

Whatever may have been Grant's reasons for not considering sitting Associate Justices, it is interesting to note that no President had appointed a sitting Justice until 1910 when President Taft appointed Associate Justice Edward D. White to become Chief Justice. Thus, during a period of 112 years, there were six Chief Justices appointed and confirmed, none of whom were sitting Justices. The next sitting Justice to become Chief was Harlan Stone, appointed by Franklin Roosevelt in 1941. This was followed by the aborted attempt of President Johnson to promote Associate Justice Abe Fortas in 1968, with the last instance being the promotion by President Reagan in 1986 of Associate Justice William H. Rehnquist to Chief Justice.

After Williams nomination was withdrawn on January 8, 1874, President Grant surprised the nation by nominating Caleb Cushing, his close friend. Cushing was seventy-four years old and had a long career in government and politics. He had been

a member of the Massachusetts Legislature, a Judge of the
Supreme Judicial Court of Massachusetts, a Member of
Congress, a General in the Mexican War, and Attorney-General
of the United States under President Grant. He also had served
in several important diplomatic posts. Most recently he had been
Chief American Counsel at the Alabama Claims Arbitration at
Geneva. This was an arbitration set up between the United States
and Great Britain to settle the disputes that had arisen over the
seizure and damages to American shipping during the Civil War.
The Arbitration results were received very favorably in the
United States. One reason given for Grant appointing Cushing
was that his British counterpart at the Geneva Arbitration had
been appointed Lord Chancellor (England's highest Judicial
office) and Grant felt that protocol required him to do the same
for Cushing by appointing him Chief Justice. One newspaper
also speculated that due to Cushing's age, Grant expected him
only to serve for a few years, and then Grant would again
appoint Williams. However, Cushing's biographer indicates that
Cushing had really coveted the position of Chief Justice. At one
time he thought he almost had it when it appeared that Chief
Justice Taney was dying during 1859 and 1860. It was
commonly thought that if the position had become vacant,
President Buchanan would have appointed Cushing.

Although the nomination of Cushing was received by
surprise by both the nation and the Senate, it was first received
quite favorably. Indeed, Cushing had just been chosen to become
Minister to Spain and this appointment had been highly
complimented by most of the Press. Prominent newspapers also
at first appeared to be pleased with his becoming Chief Justice.
The *New York Herald* wrote on January 10, 1874:

> The nomination of Caleb Cushing as Chief Justice of
> the United States . . . was yesterday's sensation in

Washington. It was a surprise to the Senate. . . .
Yet this is a nomination which amply supplies the
high acquirements demanded for the office. It is a
nomination upon which the Senate may properly
dispense with a reference to the Judiciary Committee
. . . and it is a nomination which will awaken no
opposition from any quarter, but which will
challenge the approval of intelligent men of all
parties, and will be acceptable to all sections of the
country.

The Office of Chief Justice, from the organization of
the Government under the Constitution of the United
States, has been regarded as requiring a man to fill
it, distinguished for his attainments and
comprehensive experience in the law, for his sound
judgment in his legal opinions and decisions, and for
his independence of parties and party influences, and
for a broad and lofty appreciation of his great
responsibilities. That Caleb Cushing in a
remarkable degree possesses these qualifications no
man conversant with his eventful public career -- of
the eventful period in our history of the last forty
years -- will undertake to deny. . . . He had been
a Whig, a Tyler man, a democrat and a
constitutional conservative; he was in the confidence
of President Johnson.

On the same day, the *New York Tribune* contained a story
indicating that "the nomination of Caleb Cushing . . . to be Chief
Justice of the United States was received in the Senate with
marked satisfaction." It then reported interviews with several
important Senators all predicting the quick confirmation of
Cushing. The only major newspaper to voice objection was the

New York Times which, on January 10, 1874, concluded its story on the Cushing nomination by opposing the Senate confirming him after writing that:

> Simply because he is a familiar and serviceable friend, General Grant proposes to place him at the head of the Supreme Court, to decide upon questions involving the national sovereignty and the civil rights acquired by the war and consecrated by the late amendments to the Constitution, a pro-Slavery Democrat, whose last public function was that of Franklin Pierce's Attorney-General, and whose views have been notoriously in opposition to those by virtue of which the war was carried on. Slavery was destroyed, and the rights of citizenship extended to all classes of Americans.

On the same day that Grant decided to nominate Cushing, the official notification of it was carried to the Senate and according to the biographer of Cushing, "The appointment was evidently quite unexpected to the Republican leaders, but no one had any thought that it would not be confirmed that very afternoon." Actually, the Committee on the Judiciary did recommend confirmation, but the Senate adjourned without taking any action. Over the week-end, public opinion began to change. The *New York Tribune* which had reported favorably on the previous Friday, on the following Sunday wrote:

> Its announcement on Friday afternoon was so unexpected that at first it seemed to stun people and they did not know what to say. Had a vote been reached in the Senate while the first effect of the appointment lasted, and without debate, the result would probably have been favorable for the

candidate.

The story continued by stating that although the Judiciary Committee had voted in favor of Cushing, nearly every Republican is now opposed. It quoted the remarks of some Senators that "Mr. Cushing's confirmation would be equivalent to placing the highest judicial tribunal in the land in the hands of the State Rights Democrats." Other Senators accused Cushing of selling his "legal opinions in Washington for the last twenty years . . . to whoever would pay him well for them." On the same day, the *New York Herald* ran a story with the headline "OMINOUS OPPOSITION TO THE CONFIRMATION OF CUSHING AS CHIEF JUSTICE" and commented that the Senate would again consider his appointment on Monday and "a hot conflict is expected, with what results no one pretends to know."

The most telling opposition to Cushing, however, came from the *Washington Chronicle*. As illustrated in Charles Fairman's *Mr. Justice Miller*, the *Chronicle* on Saturday, January 10, 1874, had an editorial with the headline "MAKE HASTE SLOWLY" which recalled that Cushing had agreed with the *Dred Scott* decision. The *Chronicle* continued this attack with other anti-Cushing stories. According to Cushing's biographer, "There are few instances in American history of a newspaper's pursuing a victim with such persistent malignity."

The Senate met on Monday, January 12, but after a long and bitter session postponed taking any action on Cushing until the next day. Then a most unusual event occurred.

To understand what happened, it is necessary to set forth the chronology of events that took place on Tuesday, January 13, 1874. In the morning, there was a caucus of Republican Senators that had been postponed from Monday. There was considerable discussion pro and con on whether to confirm Cushing. The Chairman of the Judiciary Committee explained the Committee's favorable report but made it clear that he no longer supported it. Senator Sargent of California bitterly opposed the nomination, but before the caucus could vote, they had to adjourn to attend the Session of the Senate. A few days previous, a Government clerk in examining a trunk full of Confederate papers had found a letter written in 1861 by Cushing to Jefferson Davis. This letter was then given to the President. In the meantime, while the Senate was in Session, the President was meeting with his Cabinet, and according to Hamilton Fish's *Diary*:

A letter was received from Senator Sargent asking for a copy of the letter. . . . The president considered that the letter could not be withheld, being on the "public files" and he authorized its release to Senator Sargent. After the Senate adjourned early Tuesday afternoon, the Republican caucus resumed its meeting. Senator Sargent then showed the letter to the other Senators. The caucus then voted to request the Judiciary to see the President and request him to withdraw Cushing's name which the President did. The content of the letter was actually innocuous. On March 21, 1861, Cushing wrote a letter to Jefferson Davis recommending a clerk in the Attorney-General's office to Davis. In it he wrote that the clerk "now resigns from his present office, from sentiments of devotion to that which alone he can feel to be his country namely; the *Confederate States* . . . I most heartily commend him . . .

Although the letter itself was not sensational, under the

temper of the times many Senators would seize the letter as a convenient excuse to reject a man who had been a Whig, a Democrat and who had allegedly been pro-slavery.

The instances of Grant's failure to get his two nominees for Chief Justice confirmed was best summed up by the *New York Herald* on January 15, 1874:

> Caleb Cushing . . . has failed to pass the ordeal of the Senate, and as in the case of Attorney-General Williams, the President's first choice, the name of the disappointed favorite has been withdrawn. In one case the professional attainments, capabilities, and experience of the man were held by a Senate largely composed of able lawyers as insufficient to meet the high requirements of the office, while in the other case the obnoxious political antecedents, opinions and affiliations were held by a Senate overwhelmingly republican as utterly disqualifying him for a loyal interpretation of the thirteenth, fourteenth and fifteenth amendments of the constitution. As a Republican the record of Williams was all that could be desired; but he failed upon his deficiencies as a lawyer and a jurist. As a lawyer and a jurist the qualification of Cushing was undisputed; but he failed upon his record as a party politician. Had Williams been as learned in the law as Cushing, or had Cushing possessed the party record of Williams, the one or the other, as the first choice of the President for Chief Justice, would doubtless have been promptly confirmed.

The nation now waited anxiously to see who would be the next nominee. The President pulled no surprises this time and nominated Morrison R. Waite of Ohio. He had been one of the counsel at the Alabama Arbitrations but did not have any previous judicial experience. The comments on this appointment were a sense of relief that an honest and non-controversial and respected lawyer was chosen. He was confirmed by a vote of sixty-three to six, and he served satisfactorily for fourteen years.

President Grant's Supreme Court Nominees

Name	Nominated	Senate Action
Ebenezer R. Hoar	12/15/1869	Rejected: 2/3/1870
Edwin M. Stanton	12/20/1869	Confirmed: 12/20/1869
William Strong	2/7/1870	Confirmed: 2/18/1870
Joseph P. Bradley	2/7/1870	Confirmed: 3/21/1870
Ward Hunt	12/3/1872	Confirmed: 12/11/1872
George H. Williams	12/1/1873	Withdrawn: 1/8/1874
Caleb Cushing	1/9/1874	Withdrawn: 1/13/1874
Morrison R. Waite	(CJ) 1/19/1874	Confirmed: 1/21/1874

Chapter Twelve

President Rutherford B. Hayes
19th President (1877-1881)
Party affiliation: Republican

Supreme Court nomination not confirmed
by the United States Senate:

STANLEY MATTHEWS
Born: July 21, 1824
Died: March 22, 1889
Education: Kenyon College,
Read law in law office
Nominated Associate Justice,
January 26, 1881
No action taken by Senate

In the election held in 1876 the Republicans nominated Rutherford Hayes, who at the time was Governor of Ohio. The Democrats nominated Samuel J. Tilden of New York. The election was close but Tilden received a majority of the popular vote. However, a few of the Southern states presented differing electoral votes, leaving the result unsettled. The provisions in the Twelfth Amendment of the Constitution were not clear on how such a dispute should be resolved. Congress therefore appointed an electoral commission consisting of eight Republicans and seven Democrats. After Hayes promised that he would withdraw all Federal troops still in the Southern states, the Commission allowed all of the disputed electoral votes to Hayes and he was elected President by one electoral vote.

This brief synopsis of the Hayes-Tilden dispute is necessary to understand the difficulty that Hayes encountered in obtaining Senate confirmation of his last Supreme Court appointment. This occurred after the resignation on January 24, 1881, of Associate Justice Noah Swayne. As President Hayes had not chosen to stand for re-election, he was a "lame duck" President to remain in office only until President-Elect Garfield was inaugurated on March 4, (the date then set for the President to take office). Although Hayes was advised to wait and let the

97

incoming President select a new Associate Justice, he decided to make his own appointment and on January 26, 1881, Hayes nominated Stanley Matthews.

Matthews was born on July 21, 1824, in Cincinnati, Ohio. After graduating from Kenyon College he studied law. In 1842, he moved to Tennessee, but in 1844 returned to Cincinnati where he practiced law and became an editor of an anti-slavery newspaper. Later, Matthews was a Trial Court Judge and then a member of the Ohio Senate, and from 1858-1861 was United States Attorney for the Southern District of Ohio. In 1877, he was appointed counsel to represent the Republican electors before the Electoral Commission. In September of the same year, the Ohio legislature chose him to become a United States Senator where he remained for two years. During that time he strongly supported a resolution favoring the restoration of the silver dollar as lawful money.

The first public reactions to Matthews' nomination for Associate Justice were mixed. The Ohio newspapers were enthusiastic and called him extremely well-qualified. Other newspapers, however, were not as favorable. There were complaints that there were already two Justices from Ohio and the *New York Times* for January 27, 1881, outlined other objections. These were:

> . . . It occurs to the mind at once that Mr. Matthews is an Ohio man, the brother-in-law and intimate personal and political friend of the President; that he was one of the counsel before the Electoral Commission, and a zealous promotor of the operations by which the difficulties in Louisiana . . . after the Electoral vote of that state had been secured were adjusted . . .

The story then condemned him for his support of the resolution that allowed the Government to use cheap silver dollars to pay off its debts. He was also criticized for his support of the railroads and other corporate interests. The article concluded by noting, "He may have been honest and conscientious in what he has done, but he has neither been judicial nor judicious . . . and [the Court] ought to be beyond the reach of calumnious attack. There should be no ground for suspicion that it can be swayed by political and personal considerations."

On January 28, the *New York Tribune* wrote that the [nomination] "is received by dismay by the public" and that "the only intelligible reason as yet known to the country for the nomination of Mr. Matthews is the fact that he is a brother-in-law of President Hayes." It then indicated that the public will accept the nomination if approved by the Judiciary Committee but there must be other reasons than Matthews' relationship to the President. As the Judiciary Committee still kept its proceedings secret, the Press had to rely on "leaks" and rumors for what was occurring in the Judiciary Committee. By February 2, it was reported that the Committee had decided to delay any consideration until the middle of February and that there was considerable concern that Matthews would favor the railroads if put on the Bench. On February 8, the New York Board of Trade and Transportation, representing 800 businesses, sent a telegram to the Judiciary Committee opposing Matthews' nomination and stating that they believed that "the great railroad corporations ... are endeavoring to obtain control of this court of last resort" against the public interests. They said that his past views made him unfit to become an Associate Justice of the Supreme Court. At the end of February, Congress adjourned without the Judiciary Committee having taken any action on Matthews.

But unlike many of the other nominees in this study,

Matthews' story had a happy ending! On March 14, 1881, President Garfield surprisingly re-nominated Matthews despite his knowledge of the deep opposition to him in the Senate. On April 11, while the nomination was still pending in the Senate, the *New York Times* published a sensational story about Matthews starting with the headline "MATTHEWS AS A SLAVE-CATCHER." Actually what the *New York Times* did was reprint a story from the *Cincinnati Commercial* of 1876 about an incident that occurred in 1858 when Matthews was a candidate for the House of Representatives. The story reported that a William Connerly, a Cincinnati local newspaper reporter, was "indicted for giving a cup of water and a crust of bread to two runaway slaves." Actually, the runaways were in Connerly's apartment resting while arrangements were being made to pass them on to the next station on the "Underground Railroad." Although Connerly became a local hero, Matthews as United States Attorney was only carrying out his sworn duty in prosecuting him under the provisions of the Fugitive Slave Act. That the *Times* would reprint this story and ignore the fact that Matthews had a distinguished anti-slavery background is an indication of the strength of the opposition that existed against Matthews.

After long and divisive debates, the Senate voted to confirm the appointment by the vote of twenty-four to twenty-three. There was considerable speculation that the Senate would vote to reconsider, but this did not happen. Matthews remains the only Justice to be confirmed by only one vote.

He served on the Court until his death in 1889 and despite all of the dire predictions of his opponents, he showed no ideological bias and frequently voted in favor of economic regulation and for labor.

Chapter Thirteen

President Grover Cleveland
22nd and 24th President (1885-1889) (1893-1897)
Party affiliation: Democrat

Supreme Court nominations not confirmed
by the United States Senate:

WILLIAM B. HORNBLOWER
Born: May 13, 1851
Died: June 16, 1914
Education: College of New Jersey
(now Princeton); Law degree,
Columbia University
Nominated Associate Justice,
   September 19, 1893
Rejected by Senate,
   January 15, 1894

WHEELER H. PECKHAM
Born: January 1, 1833
Died: September 27, 1905
Education: Albany Law School
Nominated Associate Justice,
   January 22, 1894
Rejected by Senate,
   February 16, 1894

101

Grover Cleveland was the first Democrat in the White House since James Buchanan was elected President in 1856. Cleveland also has the distinction of being the only President to have been defeated after his first term and then re-elected four years later. In his first attempt at reelection he was defeated by Benjamin Harrison in the electoral college even though he had the larger popular vote.

President Cleveland had two vacancies on the Supreme Court during his first term and both of his nominees were confirmed by the Senate. There were also two vacancies during his second term, but he had to make three nominations in order to fill the first one that occurred when Associate Justice Samuel Blatchford died in 1893. Blatchford was from New York State and it was still customary for a President to replace a Justice with one from the same state or same geographical area. Consequently, Cleveland (who was from Buffalo, New York) desired to nominate another New Yorker. He chose William B. Hornblower, a very prominent lawyer who was the acknowledged leader of the New York State Bar.

Although recognized by the Press as an excellent choice, he faced immediate difficulties in the Senate due to the exercise of "senatorial courtesy," a practice in which Senators of the same party as the President could object to Presidential nominees from the same state. According to Professor Abraham in his book on Presidential appointments, this practice started during the administration of George Washington and continues to the present, although currently it seemingly does not apply to Supreme Court nominees.

A clear example of the application of senatorial courtesy took place with the Hornblower appointment. During Cleveland's years of participation in New York Democratic politics he had clashed frequently with New York Senator David Hill who was now a powerful figure in the United States Senate. Hill regarded Hornblower as an enemy for reasons that occurred two years previous to Hornblower's nomination. At that time a colleague of Hill, Isaac Maynard, was the Deputy New York State Attorney-General and Acting Counsel for the Election Board of State Canvassers. In that capacity he was alleged to have committed a robbery of election returns that allowed for the Democratic control of the State Senate. The New York State Bar Association appointed a Committee to investigate this matter. William Hornblower was a member of this Committee which issued a scathing report that included unfavorable remarks about both Hill and Maynard. The *New York Tribune* in its preface to printing the entire report commented that:

> The Bar Association of New York . . . put upon Isaac H. Maynard the indelible brand of infamy. [The Committee] presented a report reviewing in detail his part in the theft of the State Senate in the Fall of 1891, emphatically declaring to have been "one of the gravest offense of the law," and recommending his removal from the Bench, to

which he had been appointed in reward for his crime.

When Maynard later ran for a position on the New York Court of Appeals (New York State's highest Court) he was defeated by over 100,000 votes and this defeat was credited to facts set forth in the Bar Association Report.

Despite the excellent qualifications of Hornblower, Senator Hill used his influence with the Senate and as a result, four months after the President had sent Hornblower's name to the Senate, he was denied confirmation by a vote of thirty to twenty-four.

A retrospective view of the failure of Hornblower's confirmation as Associate Justice was eloquently expressed in a Memorial that was published in the 1915 Yearbook of the Association of the Bar of the City of New York by Benjamin Cardozo, who later became a brilliant Associate Supreme Court Justice. He wrote:

In 1893 . . . when he was but forty-two years of age, President Cleveland nominated him to fill the place of Mr. Justice Blatchford on the bench of the Supreme Court of the United States. The refusal of the Senate to confirm the nomination did not dim the honor. The judgment of the bar and of the nation then was, and ever since has been, that private animosities lost to that great court a judge who would have worthily maintained the tradition of greatness. We do not need at this time to appraise the motives of those who brought that result to pass. We have merely to record the verdict which found expression . . . that the

rejection was not an estimate of fitness, but a
measure of reprisal. . . . The prize of high place
had been lost; but the greater prize of brotherly
respect and loyalty, he had made imperishably his
own.

After the rejection of Hornblower by the Senate, there
was considerable speculation as to whom the President would
nominate for the vacancy. Professor Nevins, in his biography of
Cleveland, wrote that the two New York Senators, Hill and
Murphy, had in effect informed the Nation that "no man who had
ever opposed Maynard on account of an act which was branded
as a felony by the laws should have a chance to sit in the
Supreme Court; and further, that the Senate was bound by the
rule of senatorial courtesy to make good this proclamation."
Senator Hill let it be known that he would approve the
appointment of Rufus W. Peckham, a former Justice of the New
York Court of Appeals. But Cleveland was defiant and was
determined not to let Senator Hill have his way. Instead of
nominating Rufus Peckham he nominated his brother, Wheeler H.
Peckham. This only further antagonized Hill as Wheeler
Peckham, when President of the New York State Bar
Association, had appointed the Committee that issued the
Maynard Report and had also voiced approval of the Report.

Wheeler Peckham was sixty-one years old and came from
a family of lawyers with both his father and brother having
served as judges in New York State. He studied law under his
father and also attended the Albany Law School. After practicing
law for a few years in St. Paul, Minnesota, he returned to New
York City and became a prominent corporation lawyer, mainly
representing railroads. He also participated in the prosecution of
the notorious Tweed Ring.

The nomination of Wheeler Peckham was announced on January 22, 1894, and the next day the *New York Times* had a story saying that when Senator Hill first heard of the nomination, he assumed it was for Rufus Peckham and expressed great support for him. However, when he realized that it was Wheeler Peckham and not Rufus, he issued a statement (reported in the *New York Times*) that Wheeler Peckham was possibly "the worst man who could have been appointed and is thoroughly unfitted for the position." But the *Times* also included statements from other prominent lawyers, including the Mayor of New York City, who were quoted as saying:

> It is a good appointment . . . and the nomination can not be attacked upon the ground of lack of ability.

> He is lawyer of wide experience, and stands very high in his profession.

Several others raised the question of whether or not Peckham's opposition to Maynard's elevation to the Court of Appeals would block his confirmation. But on the same day, the *New York Tribune* took a different view of the nomination when it wrote:

> By nominating Wheeler H. Peckham . . . for the vacant seat on the Supreme Court Bench President Cleveland intends to advertise his purpose to carry the New York patronage fight with Senator Hill to a further and more decisive issue, no matter the National interests may suffer or how far the dignity of the Supreme Court may be lowered by open and personal partisan wrangling over "judicial spoils." . . . Mr. Peckham appears to be exceptionally qualified to serve as a fresh red flag

flaunted in the face of Senatorial opposition, for the personal and political objections which led to Mr. Hornblower's rejection are only intensified in the record and character of the new nominee.

Despite the differing opinions of Wheeler Peckham's qualifications, the Senate on February 16, 1894, rejected Peckham by a vote of thirty-two in favor and forty-one against. The *New York Tribune* noted that ". . . no one in or out of the Administration circles seemed to have imagined that adverse majority against Hornblower would be more than doubled on today's vote." The story went on to indicate that his rejection was due to previous actions of Peckham on political and personal matters that naturally aroused a spirit of vindictiveness among many Senators.

Contemporary analysis, however, emphasized that the rejection of Hornblower and Peckham was due primarily to the Maynard affair and Senator Hill's resultant opposition. The *American Law Review*, in its January-February 1894 issue, reiterated its support of both Hornblower and Peckham, noting again the excellence of their characters and qualifications and that any allegations to the contrary were "dishonest subterfuges." The story further condemned the practice of senatorial courtesy, claiming that:

> It takes the nominating power, which the constitution has vested in the president, out of his hands, and vests it in the senators of a particular state. . . . In this way the senators wash each others' hands.

More recent research indicates, however, that while both senatorial courtesy and the Maynard Report played an important role in the rejection of both nominees, other factors were of equal importance. In an article published in 1972 in the *Tennessee Law Review* entitled "A Vacancy on the Supreme Court: The Politics of Judicial Appointment, 1893-1894," the author contends that historians have ignored the importance of political factors in the Senate's refusal to confirm Hornblower and Peckham. He indicates that in addition to the personal animosities involved, the interplay of political factors such as the differences among Democratic Senators on various issues can not be overlooked. While indeed Senator Hill may have been upset over the enmity of the President, this was not the only reason that he and his Senatorial colleagues opposed Cleveland's Supreme Court nominees. It must be remembered that at this time party discipline was expected and politicians who wanted to succeed had to be loyal to the Party leaders. Cleveland, during his years of active participation in New York Democratic activities including his terms as Mayor and Governor, tended to ignore the Party structure. Hence, there was a split between the regular Democrats and the supporters of Cleveland. The President had always acted independently of the regular Democrats and continued this policy while in the White House.

Other factors, such as Cleveland's attempt to repeal the *Silver Purchase Act* against the strenuous opposition of the Western and Southern Senators, worked against him. Another matter that caused many Republican Senators to oppose confirmation was the extreme difference of opinions between the Democratic and Republican Parties on the question of protective tariffs. The Democrats were very much opposed and the Republicans very much in favor of such a tariff. Allegations that Peckham had spoken against protective tariffs and if on the Court would vote that such tariffs were unconstitutional undoubtedly caused some Republicans who would have voted for Peckham to oppose him. It is perhaps fair to conclude that senatorial courtesy, the Maynard Report, Cleveland's unwillingness to compromise, and disagreement on economic matters all combined to defeat Cleveland's first two appointments to the Supreme Court.

But the President still had to fill the vacancy on the Court. He finally obtained Senate confirmation by nominating on February 19, 1894, Edward D. White, a Senator from Louisiana. The existing practice of the Senate never to reject one of their own resulted in White being confirmed on the same day that his name was submitted to the Senate. In 1910, he became the first Associate Justice to be promoted from the Bench to Chief Justice.

Chapter Fourteen

President Herbert C. Hoover
31st President (1929-1933)
Party affiliation: Republican

Supreme Court nomination not confirmed
by the United States Senate:

JOHN J. PARKER
Born: November 20, 1885
Died: March 17, 1958
Education: University of North
Carolina, B.A.,LL.B.
Nominated Associate Justice,
March 21, 1930
Rejected by Senate,
May 7, 1930

111

In order to fully understand the failure that President Hoover experienced with his nomination of John J. Parker for Associate Supreme Court Justice, it is necessary to examine briefly the difficulty he had in obtaining confirmation of Charles E. Hughes as Chief Justice.

When Chief Justice Taft resigned on February 3, 1930, President Hoover on the same day nominated Charles E. Hughes to replace him. Hughes had a most distinguished reputation. He was a former Governor of New York and a former Secretary of State. In 1910, President Taft had appointed him as an Associate Justice and he was quickly confirmed. In 1916 he resigned to accept the Republican nomination for President and in the election of 1916 was barely defeated by Woodrow Wilson. He subsequently became a very successful and well-known Wall Street lawyer.

The nomination of Hughes to become Chief Justice was at first received with much enthusiasm. The *New York Times* wrote that, "Never was there a clearer case of the office seeking the fit man." Newspapers throughout the country wrote editorials praising the nomination. On February 10, the Judiciary Committee issued a favorable report. Then as the nomination

113

was before the entire Senate, opposition began from a group of Progressive Republican Senators along with some Democratic Senators. The gist of their opposition was twofold. First by resigning from the Court and running for President Hughes had set a precedent that other Supreme Court Justices would be encouraged to follow. The other stated reason for the opposition was the allegation that Hughes, after returning to private practice in 1916, devoted his practice to representing wealthy corporate clients. In the words of Senator Norris, "He looks through glasses contaminated by the influence of monopoly as it seeks to get favors by means which are denied to the ordinary citizen." Although on February 13 the Senate confirmed by a vote of fifty-two to twenty-six, the attack on Hughes had a significant impact on the Senate's subsequent consideration of the nomination of John Parker.

Upon the death of Associate Justice Edward T. Sanford on March 8, 1930, President Hoover had another opportunity to appoint a Supreme Court Justice. On March 21, after receiving many recommendations from all parts of the country, President Hoover nominated John J. Parker of North Carolina, who had been a judge on the Federal Court of Appeals for the Fourth Circuit since 1925. In 1910 he had run unsuccessfully as the Republican candidate for the United States House of Representatives. In 1916 he was defeated in an election to become the Attorney-General for North Carolina. He tried again in 1920 to become the Republican Governor of North Carolina and although defeated, received more votes than any previous Republican candidate.

Before nominating him for the Supreme Court, President Hoover had considered appointing him a member of his Cabinet as Attorney-General.

On March 22, 1930, the *New York Times* ran the following:

John J. Parker of Charlotte, North Carolina, was nominated by President Hoover today to be an associate justice of the Supreme Court of the United States. . . . Only 44 years old, he is one of the youngest men ever named to the Supreme Court Bench. . . . from all indications the nomination will meet with little or no opposition in the vote on confirmation, there being no evidence of such a contest as developed over the confirmation of Chief Justice Hughes. Senators Simmons and Overman of North Carolina, although Democrats, approve the appointment strongly, while Senator Norris, chairman of the Judiciary Committee, said that as far as he knew there was but a favorable impression of Judge Parker in the Senate.

The story then noted that Attorney-General Mitchell had examined all his decisions and that he could find no cause for objection. This optimistic projection, however, did not last very long and by March 27, serious opposition began to develop. The American Federal of Labor (AFL) sent a letter to the Judiciary Committee opposing Parker's appointment due to a decision he had written, while on the Court of Appeals, upholding an anti-labor contract. On March 30, the NAACP charged Judge Parker with having flaunted provisions of the 14th and 15th Amendments of the United States Constitution.

The opposition of the AFL and other labor unions was based almost entirely on Judge Parker's opinion in the case of *International Union, United Mine Workers of America v. Red*

Jacket Consolidated Coal and Coke Co., (18 Fd 2d 839,1927). This case involved the approval by the Appellate Court of an injunction issued by a lower federal court. The issue involved was the validity of a "yellow dog" contract. Such so-called contracts were ones in which a prospective employee was required to sign an agreement promising not to join a union or to go out on strike. When unions subsequently attempted to organize at mines or factories where employees had signed such agreements, the employers would seek and obtain an injunction prohibiting the unions from engaging in organizing activities. The Supreme Court had in 1917 upheld the constitutionality of such injunctions.

Since the beginning of the twentieth century, the labor movement had been fighting the issue of labor injunctions both in Congress and in the Courts. In a statement to the Judiciary Committee, the President of the AFL indicated that:

> Labor is of the opinion that the appointment and confirmation of Judge Parker means that another injunction judge will become a member of the Supreme Court of the United States.

The other issue that played a prominent role in the developing opposition to Parker's confirmation was his statement made during his campaign for Governor of North Carolina in 1920. At the Judiciary Hearings, the NAACP stated that during the 1920 campaign, when it was claimed that the Republicans were organizing the Negro vote, Parker was quoted as having said:

> The negro as a class does not desire to enter politics. The Republican party of North Carolina does not desire him to do so. We recognize the

fact that he has not yet reached that stage in his development when he can share the burdens and responsibilities of government. This being true, and every intelligent man in North Carolina knows that it is true, the attempts of certain petty Democratic politicians to inject the race issue into every campaign is most reprehensive . . . the participation of the negro in politics is a source of evil and danger to both races and is not desired by the wise men in either race or by the Republican Party of North Carolina.

Upon inquiry by a Senator, the spokesman for the NAACP said that he did not personally know Judge Parker and the quoted statement was the sole reason for the stated opposition. Both the opposition and supporters of Parker continued to grow and many pages of the *Congressional Record* were filled with Senators either favoring or refuting the alleged anti-labor or anti-Negro position of Judge Parker. The best way to trace the progress of the confirmation is to see how it developed chronologically as reported in the *New York Times*.

March 22 John J. Parker, a Republican, nominated as Associate Justice of Supreme Court. Little or no opposition expected.

March 25 Nomination referred to Senate Judiciary Committee

March 26 AFL opposes nomination because of decision upholding "yellow dog' labor contracts ... Asks Senate Judiciary Committee to study his rulings.

March 29 Union labor opposes appointment.

April 1   Opposition and supporters line up for fight over confirmation.

April 6   Legal comment on "yellow-dog" labor contracts.

April 12   President Hoover told by an administration spokesman that opposition was growing among Republican Senators who have large Negro populations in their states and are up for re-election. . . . Calls attention to Negro alarm over Parker's 1920 remarks. President agrees to investigate. . . . Parker's decision that invalidated a Richmond, Virginia, ordinance for segregation has caused several southern Democratic Senators to drop their support for Parker. . . . In defense of Parker it is claimed that he was only following Supreme Court precedent in the "yellow-dog" decision. . . . Favorable Subcommittee report predicted. . . . Memorandum from Attorney-General explains and defends the "yellow dog" decision and emphasizes Hoover's support.

April 14   Editorial quoting President Hoover that he will not withdraw Judge Parker's nomination. President refers to anti-Parker arguments as being wholly "extraneous." They do not, he says, go to the question of Judge Parker's ability or character.

April 16   Judiciary members opposed to Parker are considering an investigation of what they consider "propaganda" in favor of his confirmation and are considering calling him to appear before the committee for an examination into his so-called "yellow dog" contract decision. . . . NAACP writes letter to President Hoover asking him to withdraw nomination citing an article from the Greensboro (N.C.) *Daily News* in 1920 quoting Judge Parker as having said that Negroes were not sufficiently developed to share governmental responsibilities and that their participation in politics "is a source of evil and danger to both parties." The letter goes on to say, concerning the alleged quotation, that if Judge Parker meant what he said (and he had not denied it), it is obvious that he is not qualified for the Supreme Court. If however he said it but did not believe it, he is more unfit by appealing to racial prejudice for political advantage.

April 17   President Hoover makes it clear that he has no intention of withdrawing the nomination. Republican Senators from South propose secret vote. Republican Senator from Missouri makes public a telegram sent to the President that confirmation would be an affront to Negroes and would cause Republicans to lose the next few elections in Missouri,

April 18   Seventeen Republican Senators, led by Republican floor leader, declare their opposition to Judge Parker's nomination. A White House spokesman indicates that nothing has developed against Parker's qualifications and that the protests are based upon political considerations and not the legal ability of the nominee.

April 19   Judiciary Committee to ask Judge Parker to appear and to reply to the attacks made against him.

April 20   Parker indicates his willingness to appear before the Committee; additional Senators declare opposition to confirmation.

April 22   The Judiciary Committee votes ten to six to reject Parker's confirmation; after a long debate, Committee had previously by a vote of ten to four decided not to invite Parker to appear before the Committee. President Hoover indicates continuing support for Judge Parker . . . action has disturbed Southern Democratic Senators who fear if they vote against

Parker any one who holds that Negroes are not yet ready for leadership in political affairs is not entitled to be on the Supreme Court. Not for a long time has the serenity of the Senate been so disturbed as by the case of Judge John J. Parker. . . . Coming on top of the resistance in the Senate to the confirmation of Chief Justice Hughes, opinion on Parker's nomination has indicated that a small but active group of Senators intend to block every Supreme Court appointment where the nominee's judicial or legal tendencies do not conform to that degree of "liberalism" which this group contends needs more generally in its personnel.

April 28   Judge Parker defends himself in letter to Judiciary Committee. In regard to the allegations of AFL criticizing his decision in the *Red Jacket* case, he insists that he only followed the precedents of the Supreme Court. In regard to the opposition expressed by the NAACP, he writes, "I regard the Constitution and all its amendments as the fundamental and supreme law of the land . . . the effort to interpret some statement alleged to have been made ten years ago in a speech as indicating a contrary disposition is wholly unjustified."

April 29   Senator Borah opens fight in Senate claiming that Parker is opposed to labor; Senator Overman (North Carolina) opens defense of Parker.

April 30   Debates continue in Senate.

May 2   Debate in the Senate . . . grows heated . . . as Senator Fess of Ohio criticizes the "manufactured clamor" of the opposition, a charge that aroused both Senators Borah and Johnson, who retort that the propaganda is not one-sided and declare that proponent "propagandists" are plainly demanding Judge Parker's confirmation to make North Carolina a Republican state.

May 3   Senator Norris closes Senate debate for opposition.

May 4   Rumors of patronage pressure made by proponents.

May 5   Backers to gain additional support. Senator Ashurst charges federal judgeships and other appointments are offered to Parker's backers; various other charges made by proponents and opponents.

May 8   Senate rejects Judge Parker, 41 to 39; spirited attack by Johnson precedes final vote.

Examining the rejection of Judge Parker with the advantage of over sixty years hindsight, several factors can now be observed that were perhaps not apparent in 1930. The changing economic scene in the movement to restrain unregulated economic activities was reflected in various ways during the early years of the twentieth century. Among these were President Theodore Roosevelt's fight against unrestrained capitalism and the growth of the Progressive Party under the Wisconsin LaFollettes. As a result, the economic views of Supreme Court nominees became more important than their political affiliations. This became apparent during the Senate debates as exemplified by the following dialogue that occurred during the consideration of Parker on May 1:

> **Senator Norris:** I am frank to admit that I want to see men put on the Supreme Bench who are not so encrusted with ancient theories that they are to inflict human slavery upon us now.
>
> **Senator Allen:** By modern ideas you mean your own ideas?

Senator Norris: Yes, I do.

It is also important to recall that until 1916 there were not any public records of the proceedings of the Judiciary Committee or the Senate on what occurred in regard to Supreme Court nominees. Also it was not until 1913 that the Seventeenth Amendment of the Constitution was adopted which provided for the direct election of Senators. Both of these factors politicized the confirmation process by making Senators much more sensitive to pressure groups.

Another matter that undoubtedly had an important impact on Parker's rejection was the economic situation in 1930. The stock market had crashed on October 1929, and the country was entering the first phase of the Great Depression of the 1930's. Although the market partially recovered in the early part of 1930, by the end of the year the market again plunged; factories started closing and breadlines grew longer. All of this must have been apparent to those Senators who were up for re-election in 1930. And events proved them right as the Republicans lost eight seats in that election.

An ironic aspect of this rejection is that although the labor movement and the NAACP in defeating Parker illustrated the important role that they and other groups now have, Parker would have been better for them than the one who was appointed in his place, Justice Owen J. Roberts. Judge Parker remained on the Court of Appeals and consistently upheld New Deal legislation while Justice Roberts became one of the conservatives on the Supreme Court.

Chapter Fifteen

President Lyndon B. Johnson
36th President (1963-1969)
Party affiliation: Democrat

Supreme Court nominations not confirmed
by the United States Senate:

ABE FORTAS
Born: June 19, 1910
Died: April 5, 1982
Education: B.A. Southwestern
College; LL.B. Yale University
Appointed Associate Justice,
August 11, 1965
Nominated Chief Justice,
June 26, 1968
Withdrawn, October 4, 1968
Resigned as Associate Justice,
May 14, 1969

HOMER THORNBERRY
Born: January 9, 1909
Died:
Education: B.B.A., LL.B University
of Texas, Austin
Nominated Associate Justice,
June 26, 1968
Withdrawn, October 4, 1968

123

During the first sixty-seven years of the twentieth century, Presidents had nominated and received confirmation for forty-two appointments to the Supreme Court, with Judge Parker's being the only nomination turned down by the Senate between 1894 and 1968. This led one author writing in 1965 to comment that, "Rejection by the Senate is unlikely, and in this century has proven to be almost impossible." (S. Krislov, *Supreme Court in the Political Process*.) But this prediction was proven wrong after only three years when the nomination of Associate Justice Abe Fortas to become Chief Justice ran into difficulty with the Senate.

To understand what happened it is necessary to examine briefly the career of President Lyndon Johnson.

In 1937, Johnson was elected to the United States House of Representatives and became supportive of President Roosevelt's New Deal Programs. In 1948, a United States Senate seat from Texas became vacant and Johnson decided to become a candidate for it. At this time Texas, as most Southern states, was a one-party state where victory in the Democratic primary election assured victory in the regular Fall election. Johnson's opponent in the Texas Democratic primary election

125

was Coke Stevenson, a very popular former Governor. The ensuing campaign was a long and bitter one. In the July primary election Stevenson received forty percent of the vote and Johnson thirty-four percent. As neither candidate received a majority, under Texas law there had to be a run-off election on May 24. As the ballots were being counted for this election, the lead shifted back and forth and it took several days before the final count was recorded, showing Stevenson the victor by 114 votes. But the very next day news came that in the small town of Alice in the Texas panhandle, 202 uncounted votes were discovered, with 201 being for Johnson. Supporters of Johnson then were able to obtain the endorsement of the state Democratic Party. Stevenson then obtained an injunction from a Federal District Court Judge prohibiting the placing of Johnson's name on the November ballot.

Johnson called upon Abe Fortas, a prominent Washington lawyer, for advice and help. Fortas was a graduate of the Yale Law School where he had become a protege of William Douglas (a future Supreme Court Justice) who obtained for him positions in various federal agencies. By 1948, Fortas was partner in a prestigious Washington law firm. As the United States Supreme Court was in its summer recess, Fortas went before Justice Hugo Black and convinced him to overturn the injunction against Johnson's name being on the November ballot. Thus Johnson became a United States Senator and became known as "Landslide" Johnson!

Senator Johnson had a distinguished career in the Senate, eventually becoming the Senate Majority Leader. In 1960, he was elected Vice-President and became President after the assassination of President Kennedy in November 1963. During his years in the Senate and as President, he remained thankful for what Fortas had done for him in connection with the Texas

Senate race. They became close friends and Fortas became Johnson's confidential advisor.

Johnson believed that Fortas should become a Supreme Court Justice, as he truly felt that Fortas deserved this honor. Additionally, Johnson wanted to make sure that he would have a Justice on the Court who could be counted on to support his policies. Although Fortas had repeatedly told him that he had absolutely no interest in joining the Supreme Court, Johnson remained determined to appoint him at his first opportunity. All biographers of Lyndon Johnson emphasize how strong-minded he was and how he eventually obtained what he wanted. When Adlai Stevenson who was Ambassador to the United Nations died in 1965, Johnson saw his opportunity to create a vacancy on the Court for Fortas. He accomplished this by cajoling Justice Arthur J. Goldberg to resign his seat on the Court and to replace Adlai Stevenson at the United Nations. Johnson offered the vacant Court position to Fortas who declined, indicating his desire to stay with his law firm.

But Johnson was determined to have his way. The President had a press conference scheduled for July 28, and that morning he telephoned Fortas and requested him to join him at the press conference. When Fortas met with Johnson at the White House prior to the press conference, the President told Fortas that he was going to announce that he was sending 50,000 more troops to Vietnam. Johnson then added, "I want you to go on the Supreme Court." Fortas was trapped and once again President Johnson obtained what he wanted.

After Johnson's announcement on Vietnam, he informed the press that he was appointing Fortas to take Goldberg's place on the Supreme Court. He said that Fortas was his first choice and he was "a scholar, a profound thinker, a lawyer of superior ability and a man humane and deeply compassionate toward his fellow man." He then stated that it is well-known that Fortas did not seek the appointment and this was a case of the job seeking the man.

The President sent Fortas' name to the Senate on July 28, 1965. Although in general his nomination was greeted affirmatively, some Senators were troubled by Fortas' close relationship with President Johnson. While testifying before the Senate Judiciary Committee, Senator Hruska questioned Fortas about this matter:

> **Senator Hruska.** Now there is another proposition that has been widely discussed. Through the years you have formed a very close friendship and relationship with our President, which is not merely personal and social; it has also involved professional, business and political dealings including many personal transactions with the President's own estate, and so on. In the President we not only have a man whom you have represented and for whom you have apparently great affection and respect; we also have a man in the political world who is espousing a particular kind of political and legislative program.
>
> I presume in due time various aspects of this administration's program will wind up before the Supreme Court of the United States. ... [I]s there anything in your relationship with the President that would militate in any way against your being able to sit on that bench and pass judgment on cases that come along and that would affect your ability to function in the true fashion and tradition?

Mr. Fortas. The short answer to that, Senator, is absolutely not, but let me say to you that there are two things that have been vastly exaggerated out of all connection with reality. One is the extent to which I am a Presidential advisor, and the other is the extent to which I am a proficient violinist.... You know, Senator, I did not want any public position, and I made that clear to him. . . . But I am very distressed at any suggestion or idea that any relationship that I might have with the President would in any way bear upon the discharge of my functions in the Court. It could not be.

With that assurance, the Judiciary Committee unanimously endorsed Fortas and on August 11, 1965, the Senate by voice vote confirmed his appointment as an Associate Justice.

Despite this testimony President Johnson still requested advice from Fortas, who could not resist giving it. As the Johnson Administration began to lose its popularity and as the country became more and more divided over Vietnam, Johnson increasingly sought advice from Fortas until by early 1968 he was meeting frequently with the President and his advisors in the White House.

President Johnson was defeated by Eugene McCarthy in the New Hampshire Democratic primary, and, on March 31, 1968, shocked the Nation by announcing that he would not stand for reelection.

Early in June 1968, Chief Justice Warren informed President Johnson that he intended to retire as provided for by a federal statute that allowed federal justices and judges to retire from active duty but to continue receiving their full salary. Warren's formal letter to the President merely stated that "... I hereby advise you of my intention to retire as Chief Justice of the United States effective at your pleasure." In an accompanying letter, the Chief Justice wrote that his main reason for retiring was his advanced age (seventy-seven) and that "I, therefore, conceive it to be my duty to give way to someone who will have more years ahead to cope with the problems which will come before the Court." The President in return sent a very friendly letter in which he wrote that "... [h]owever, in deference to your wishes, I will seek a replacement to fill the vacancy in the office of Chief Justice that will be occasioned when you depart. With your agreement, I will accept your decision to retire effective at such time as a successor is qualified."

While Earl Warren never did explain what influenced him to plan to retire at this particular time, one biographer (Robert Shogun) has a very feasible explanation. By June 1968, it was widely expected that the Republicans would win in the forthcoming presidential election and that the Republican candidate would most likely be Richard Nixon. Although both Warren and Nixon were Republicans from California, they had always been political enemies. Warren most likely was fearful that if he waited to retire until after the election, Nixon would choose a Chief Justice who would lead the Court in a different direction than the Warren Court had taken.

Upon receiving Warren's intention to retire, Johnson immediately seized the opportunity to nominate his old and admired friend, Abe Fortas, to become Chief Justice. As this would require a replacement for Fortas' seat as Associate Justice, he also nominated an old Texas friend, Homer Thornberry, who was a judge on the Federal Court of Appeals for the Fifth Circuit. On June 26, 1968, both names were sent to the Senate.

President Johnson had previously consulted with the Senate Majority Leader as well as the Republican Minority Leader and they had assured him they would support the confirmation of both Fortas and Thornberry. President Johnson may have thought that he would have no trouble obtaining the consent of the Senate, but events turned out differently. The *New York Times* in an editorial on June 30 wrote that:

> President Johnson has made two good choices for the high court. For although both are old Presidential cronies, they are also appointees of quality. No one can predict how a man will behave on the bench when it comes to deciding constitutional issues. But this much is certain: There is a basis for hope that, like Chief Justice Warren, they can grow in stature in this historic branch of government. . . ."

However, President Johnson should have been alerted that the confirmation of Fortas would not receive smooth sailing in the Senate. On June 21, five days before Johnson sent the names of Fortas and Thornberry to the Senate, Senator Griffin, a Republican from Michigan, in a Senate speech said:

> An unconfirmed report has been circulating this morning that Chief Justice Earl Warren has submitted his resignation.
>
> Rumors appeared in print earlier this week to the effect that the Chief Justice might make such a move so that President Johnson could designate the next Chief Justice of the Supreme Court. . . .
> I want to indicate emphatically, as one U.S. Senator, that I shall not vote to confirm an

appointment by a "lame duck" President.

If a "lame duck" President should seek at this stage to appoint the leadership of the Supreme Court for many years in the future, I believe he would be breaking faith with our system and that such a move would be an affront to the American people.

The same day that the nominations went to the Senate, nineteen out of thirty-two Republican Senators issued a statement that would oppose any nomination of the President due to his "lame duck" status. Additionally, several Southern Democratic Senators who had strongly protested against the civil rights decisions of the Warren Court also announced their opposition to Fortas.

The Judiciary Committee opened hearings on July 11, 1968, and met for eleven days during July and September. Fortas appeared before the Committee, becoming the first nominee for Chief Justice ever to appear before the Judiciary Committee. The printed records of the Hearings consist of over 1400 pages!

Although the American Bar Association gave Fortas a "highly qualified rating," many witnesses testified against his confirmation. In addition to the argument that President Johnson should leave the appointment to the next President, more substantive reasons for opposing the nomination were given to the Committee.

One objection was the allegation that there was not a vacancy to be filled. The President had written to Warren that "I will accept your decision to retire effective at such time as a successor is qualified." The question was raised as to whether the Senate had the power to confirm a nominee unless the incumbent had specified a day certain to retire. Undoubtedly the President and Warren chose this method so that if the Senate refused to confirm Fortas, then Warren would stay on as Chief Justice. What this did was to inform Warren's detractors in the Senate to either confirm Fortas or continue to have Warren as Chief Justice. In a press interview reprinted in the Judiciary Committee report, Warren is quoted as saying that he would stay on as Chief Justice if Fortas were not confirmed.

The Judiciary Committee requested the Justice Department's opinion on whether a vacancy did exist on the Court. The Justice Department submitted a memorandum upholding the validity of Fortas' nomination by citing as precedent instances where previous Presidents had used similar arrangements in making judicial appointments. While Senator Ervin of North Carolina spent considerable time cross-examining Attorney-General Ramsey Clark and arguing that no vacancy would exist until Warren actually retired, the Judiciary Committee accepted the conclusions of the Justice Department.

Considerable time was expended by some Senators in questioning Fortas on how he would decide certain hypothetical cases. Fortas took the position that he could not comment on cases that may some day come before the Court. This did not stop Senator Ervin who one day spent over two hours questioning Fortas, with Fortas repeating that he could not comment on such cases. When the Chairman directly asked Fortas: "To what extent ... do you believe that the Court should attempt to bring about social, economic, or political changes?" Fortas replied, "Zero, absolutely zero."

Nevertheless, some Senators continued to examine and

criticize Fortas for his opinions on obscenity, although he had actually joined the majority in which the Court had upheld a conviction in an obscenity case for the first time in ten years.

But perhaps the most substantial charges made against Fortas dealt with his close and personal relationship with the President. Although this matter had been raised during the Confirmation hearings of Fortas as Associate Justice in 1965, he was again closely questioned about his relation with the President. It was charged that Fortas had written speeches and drafted legislation for the President. Fortas admitted that he had attended strategy meetings at the White House, mostly involving Vietnam and the riots that were taking place in some cities. He insisted, however, that the President never asked him anything that would conflict with his judicial duties and if anything did come before the Court that might cause a conflict of interest, he would not sit on that case. He also called to the Committee's attention the fact that many previous Presidents, starting with George Washington, had sought the advice of sitting Supreme Court Justices. The question, however, was whether Fortas in his relationship with the President had crossed the line that should exist between the President and the Judiciary. Undoubtedly many Senators felt that Fortas did go beyond the separation of power provisions of the Constitution.

The President and the Chairman of the Judiciary committee had hoped to bring the nominations before the full Senate before it adjourned for the month of August. Those opposing the nominations were successful, however, in postponing the Hearing until September.

When the Judiciary Committee reconvened in September, another disturbing factor about Fortas was brought to the Committee's attention. During the summer Fortas had given a series of seminars at the School of Law of American University. While it is not unusual for a Supreme Court Justice to lecture at a law school, Fortas' arrangement was different. It turned out that Fortas was paid $15,000 for the seminars. This seemed unusually high considering that his salary at that time was $39,500. Moreover, Fortas was not being paid from University funds but from money raised by Paul Porter, Fortas' former law partner, who obtained the money from five wealthy heads of corporations who were all clients of Fortas' former law firm.

On September 17, the Judiciary Committee finally approved the confirmation of Fortas by a vote of eleven to six. On September 25, the full Senate had before it the motion to confirm the nomination of Abe Fortas for Chief Justice of the United States. During July, there had been frequent debate on the floor of the Senate over the Fortas nomination, with Senators in favor insisting that there was no such thing as a "lame duck" President, as the Constitution gives the incumbent President full power to act as President until his successor is sworn in. Those opposed continued to criticize Fortas for his liberal opinions and for his close relationship with the President. When the question was before the full Senate, it became clear that although a majority of the Senators would vote for confirmation, the opponents intended to filibuster to prevent the taking of a vote. For example, Senator Griffin spoke for three days and other Senators continued the filibuster. On October 1, a motion was made to limit debate but it failed to pass. The next day Fortas asked the President to withdraw his name and the President on October 4 sent a message to the Senate withdrawing the names of Fortas and Thornberry. This was the first time that a filibuster had ever been used to prevent the Senate from voting on the confirmation of a Supreme Court nominee.

This, however, is not the end of the saga of the Fortas

nomination as Chief Justice. After the President withdrew his name, Fortas remained on the Bench as an Associate Justice. On May 5, 1969, Fortas once again became headline news when *Life* magazine published an article entitled "The Justice ... and the Stock Manipulator." It claimed that, while an Associate Justice, Fortas had received $20,000 from the Wolfson Family Foundation.

Louis Wolfson was a wealthy financier and had formed a charitable foundation devoted to the study of juvenile delinquency. In 1966, while Fortas was on the Bench, he was contacted by Wolfson and asked to join the Board of Directors of his Foundation. Fortas agreed and signed a contract with the Foundation in which he was to receive $20,000 a year for life, and his wife was to continue to receive this sum for her life if she outlived Fortas. Fortas received his first check in early 1966 but in December returned it after Wolfson was indicted for selling unregistered stock. After the story was published in *Life*, a clamor arose, both in and out of Congress, for the impeachment of Fortas. Although Fortas maintained that he had done nothing wrong, he resigned on May 14, 1969, stating that although "[t]here had been no default in the performance of my judicial duties" he was resigning for "the welfare and maximum effectiveness of the Court."

The withdrawal of Associate Justice Fortas' name for appointment as Chief Justice had effectively eliminated any seat on the Court for Judge Thornberry.

During the Senate Judiciary Committee Hearings on the nomination of Thornberry, the only substantial objection raised as to his qualifications was the charge of cronyism. *Webster's Ninth New Collegiate Dictionary* defines this as "partiality to cronies esp. as evidenced in the appointment of political-hangers-on to office without regard to their qualifications."

Thornberry was indeed a long-standing friend of President Johnson. They were both from Austin, Texas, and Thornberry was elected to Congress from the same District that Johnson had held. But Thornberry was not a "hanger-on" without qualifications of his own, having served as both a Federal District Judge and Judge of the Court of Appeals. The Standing Committee on the Federal Judiciary of the American Bar Association gave Thornberry its "highly acceptable" rating, and it is generally agreed that if the Senate had confirmed Fortas as Chief Justice, it would also have confirmed Thornberry as Associate Justice.

Chapter Sixteen

President Richard M. Nixon
37th President (1969-1974)
Party affiliation: Republican

Supreme Court nominations not confirmed
by the United States Senate:

CLEMENT HAYNSWORTH, JR.
Born: October 30, 1912
Died:
Education: Furman University;
    LL.B., Harvard University
Nominated Associate Justice,
    August 18, 1969
Rejected by Senate,
    November 21, 1969

G. HARROLD CARSWELL
Born: December 22, 1919
Died: July 31, 1992
Education: Duke University;
    LL.B., Mercer University
Nominated Associate Justice,
    January 19, 1970
Rejected by Senate,
    April 8, 1970

After Abe Fortas' nomination for Chief Justice was withdrawn on October 4, 1968, President Johnson made no further nominations. In November, Richard Nixon was elected President of the United States, and was inaugurated on January 20, 1969. Earl Warren remained as Chief Justice until his resignation became effective on June 23, 1969. On May 21, 1969, Nixon nominated Warren E. Burger as Chief Justice and he was confirmed by the Senate on June 9, 1969. There was still another vacant seat on the Supreme Court due to the resignation of Associate Justice Fortas. On August 18, 1969, Nixon nominated Clement Haynsworth, Jr. to fill the vacated Fortas seat.

Haynsworth was from South Carolina and President Eisenhower in 1957 had appointed him to the Federal Court of Appeals for the Fourth Circuit. In 1964, he became Chief Judge of that Court. President Nixon's appointment of one from South Carolina was seen by many observers to be part of his "Southern strategy." Since the Supreme Court had held school segregation unconstitutional in 1954, and the Democratic Party was increasingly controlled by its liberal wing, Southern states that for many years had been solidly Democratic were beginning to support Republican candidates. It was thought that President

141

Nixon was encouraging this trend by proposing legislation favored by Southern members of the Congress and by appointing Southerners to important positions in his administration.

When the *New York Times* first reported the nomination on August 18, it indicated that Haynsworth was Nixon's choice because, in addition to wanting a Southern Republican, he also wished to make the Supreme Court more conservative. It was also suggested that early confirmation by the Senate was expected. To Nixon's regret, this was not to be the case. Almost immediately, objections were raised against Haynsworth by the NAACP, claiming that he had voted against a court-ordered school desegregation by a lower Federal Court. Other civil rights organizations also opposed his appointment, claiming that he had as a judge consistently taken anti-civil rights positions. On August 21, the *New York Times* reported that the AFL-CIO would oppose Haynsworth, as his record on the U.S. Court of Appeals showed that he was "hostile to workers and Negroes." Labor leaders also charged that in one instance Haynsworth ruled against a labor union while he was on the Board of Directors of the company involved in the litigation. But then more serious allegations were made. It was charged that Haynsworth had participated in court decisions involving corporations in which he held stock.

When the Senate Judiciary Committee began hearings on September 16, 1969, they were concerned with these issues: whether Haynsworth acted unethically, his judicial philosophy, and his labor decisions.

Title 28 of the *United States Code* §§455 provides as follows:

Any justice or judge of the United States shall

disqualify himself in any case in which he has a
substantial interest . . . or is so related to or
connected with any party or his attorney as to
render it improper, in his opinion, for him to sit
on the trial, appeal, or other proceedings therein.

At the time of Haynsworth's nomination, Canon 29 of the
America Bar Association Canons of Judicial Ethics provided that:

A judge should abstain from performing or taking
part in any judicial act in which his personal
interests are involved.

It was alleged by opponents of Haynsworth that he should
have disqualified himself from several cases he heard as a
member of the Court of Appeals for the Fourth Circuit. Among
these was a case in which the Court of Appeals ruled against a
National Labor Relations Board decision in favor of the Textile
Workers of America. The Union claimed that Haynsworth had
joined in a Fourth Circuit opinion favorable to a company in
which Haynsworth had been a member of the Board of Directors.
The Union claimed that Haynsworth should have disqualified
himself from hearing this case.

Another instance for which Haynsworth was criticized was
for hearing a case in which one of the litigants had a subsidiary
corporation in which he held stock.

As both the *United States Code* provision and the
American Bar Association Canons use language general in nature,
Senators and other witnesses spent considerable time debating
whether the specific facts of Haynsworth's actions in any way
violated the intent of the Statute or the Canon. The majority
members of the Judiciary Committee voted, after an extensive

discussion of the facts, that Judge Haynsworth did not in any way act unethically.

In its Report, the Committee wrote:

> . . . [T]he committee has concluded that so-called "ethics" attacks against Judge Haynsworth have not been substantiated, and that nothing in his judicial conduct during the 12 years he has sat as judge in the Court of Appeals for the Fourth Circuit would in any way justify recommending against his confirmation. . . ."

Both the Judiciary Committee and the Senate as a whole, in addition to debating whether Judge Haynsworth met the high ethical standards required of Judges, also focused part of their debate on Haynsworth's judicial philosophy. The Senators were divided on this issue. Some argued that only the professional qualifications of a nominee should be considered, while others claimed that a nominee's philosophical convictions do not represent a reason for rejection. The case for not considering a nominee's philosophy was articulated in the Judiciary Committee's Hearings by Senator Hruska when he pointed to the example of the Senate's confirmation of Thurgood Marshall:

> He was by no means a nonpartisan person in the field of civil rights litigation. He was quite partisan and yet this committee felt that he was a man of judicial temperament. He was a man of integrity. He was a man who was successful in the practice. While it is true the bulk of it had to do with a certain field of the law we nevertheless approved him regardless of his political philosophy and his efforts along a certain line. We said that

none of that is our business. That is the
President's business. . . .

A further statement of this view was expressed by Senator
Tydings while questioning a witness before the Judiciary
Committee:

Senator Tydings: Would it be a fair statement to
say that not just the great weight but the
overwhelming opinion of the lawyers of Maryland
who have had contact, direct or indirect, with
Judge Haynsworth would be that he, regardless of
his political philosophy or political allegiance or
political registration, is competent and qualified to
be a Justice of the Supreme Court?

Witness (President of Maryland Bar Association):
I believe that is correct. . . .

The opposite point of view can be ascertained by questions
Senator Kennedy asked of the Chairman of the American Bar
Association Committee on Judicial Standards during his testimony
before the Judiciary Committee:

Senator Kennedy: I am just wondering, in your
own considerations of the qualifications of the
candidate for the Supreme Court, do you make
any, or attempt to make any, kind of evaluation as
to whether the candidate is a contemporary man of
the times, whether he has any real kind of
appreciation for the various forces or factors
which are relevant in a rapidly moving society?

Witness: . . . if we disagree with (a candidate's)

views, political, sociological, or otherwise, we would not regard that as a factor with us. We think once a man [sic] is qualified professionally, these other matters are for the President to be selective about. . . .

On November 12, 1969, the Judiciary Committee issued its report on Clement F. Haynsworth, Jr. By a vote of eleven to seven it recommended the confirmation of Judge Haynsworth as Associate Justice of the Supreme Court of the United States.

On November 14, 1969, the Senate opened debate on the confirmation of Haynsworth and on November 21, 1969, voted 55-45 to refuse confirmation, with seventeen Republican Senators, including the Assistant Republican Minority leader, joining in the majority vote. Some Senators voted against confirmation because they felt that even if Haynsworth did not technically breach any ethical standards, the Canon of Judicial Ethics statements that a judge should avoid any conduct that would justify the impression or give any suspicion that a judge had acted improperly prohibited them from voting for his confirmation. Other Senators voted against him due to what they considered to be his anti-civil rights and anti-labor decisions. There was probably another underlying cause for the majority vote. Some Senators undoubtedly felt that after refusing to confirm Justice Fortas as Chief Justice on ethical grounds, it would be hypocritical to confirm Haynsworth after similar ethical matters had been raised about him. Other Senators undoubtedly voted against confirmation as a matter of revenge for the treatment of Justice Fortas. On the day after the rejection, the *Washington Post* commented in an editorial that:

The rejection, despite the speeches and the comments on Capitol hill to the contrary, seems to have resulted more from ideological and plainly political considerations than from ethical ones. It is impossible to believe that all Northern liberals and all Southern conservatives have such dramatically different ethical standards.

President Nixon was upset with the Senate's rejection and on the same day issued a statement in which he said:

I deeply regret this action. I believe a majority of the people in the nation regret it . . .

When the current Congress returns for its second session in January I will nominate another Associate Justice. The criteria I shall apply for this selection will be consistent with my commitments to the American people before my election as President a year ago.

After the Senate refused to confirm the appointment of Judge Haynsworth, President Nixon had to make another nomination to fill the seat vacated by the resignation of Associate Justice Abe Fortas. He was still determined to nominate another Southerner. After receiving many suggestions from different sources, he made the surprising announcement on January 19, 1970, that he was nominating G. Harrold Carswell of Tallahassee, Florida. In 1948, Carswell had been appointed Chief Judge of the United States District Court for the Northern District of Florida, and in June he was appointed to the Federal Court of Appeals for the Fifth Circuit.

There was the general expectation that Carswell would be confirmed without any trouble. It was anticipated that the last thing the Senate would want would be another grueling confirmation battle after what they went through with Haynsworth and Fortas. Immediately after the President's announcement, there were expressions of support from the two Florida Senators and several prominent jurists. The American Bar Association called him "qualified" (at the time, the American Bar Association only indicated that a nominee was either unqualified or qualified). But within days after the nomination, signs began to appear that indicated that Carswell's confirmation would not proceed without difficulties. On January 21, the *New York Times* in an editorial opposing the nomination wrote that the President seemingly intended to "lower the significance of the Court by the appointment of an incompetent." On January 25, a letter was printed in which the writer claimed that Judge Carswell made persistent attempts to impede Negro registration. But the most sensational item appeared in a story on January 22 in the *Washington Post*, which reprinted a speech made in 1948 by Carswell when he was campaigning for a seat in the Georgia legislature. During this speech, after calling the proposed Civil Rights Program the "Civil Wrongs Program," he went on to say:

> I am a Southern by ancestry, birth, training, inclination, belief and practice. I believe that segregation of the races is proper and the only practical and correct way of life in our states. I have always so believed and I shall always so act. I shall be the last to submit to any attempt on the part of anyone to break down and to weaken this firmly established policy of our people.

> If my own brother were to advocate such a program, I would be compelled to take issue and to oppose him to the limits of my ability.

> I yield to no man as a fellow candidate, or as a

fellow citizen, in the firm, vigorous belief in the principle of white supremacy, and I shall always be so governed.

As a result of the publication of this story, the NAACP issued a statement urging his rejection. The *New York Times* carried a story stating that by this appointment Nixon expressed a desire to appeal to "middle America" and that it was part of his "Southern Strategy."

On January 27, 1970, the Judiciary Committee began its Hearings, which would last for five full days, on the Carswell appointment. One of the first questions asked of Judge Carswell was the matter of his speech in 1948 upholding white supremacy, and he was asked if he had indeed made that speech. He replied that he had no present recollection of it and that he would not contradict the story that appeared in the press. He then went on to state that "those words themselves are obnoxious and abhorrent to me. I am not a racist. I have no notions, secretive, open, or otherwise, of racial superiority. . . ." Carswell went on to emphasize that he was only twenty-eight years old when he had made that speech.

Further trouble was in store for him during his first day of testimony. On January 26, the day before the hearings began, the *Washington Post* carried a story about the Tallahassee Golf Club and Carswell's role in it while he was an United States Attorney. According to the story, the Golf Club was a public one owned by the City. The United States Supreme Court had previously held that it was unconstitutional for a city to operate a municipal golf course that denied access to Negroes. Several citizens then arranged to lease the golf course from the City. In order to accomplish this a corporation was formed, and Carswell was listed as one of the original incorporators. The purpose of this was to maintain the golf course as a segregated facility. When questioned about this by one of the Senators, Carswell admitted of having been a member at one time but said, "I was never an officer or director of any country club anywhere."

As the Hearings continued, several witnesses testified that Carswell while a Judge on the Federal District Court expressed his dislike for Northern civil right lawyers coming into Florida. Still other lawyers claimed that Judge Carswell had been rude and antagonistic to Negro lawyers who appeared before him. Additional witnesses came before the Committee, some testifying in favor of Carswell, some testifying in opposition. One reason given by those against the confirmation of Carswell was succinctly presented by Joseph L. Rauh, Jr., appearing on behalf of the Leadership Conference of Civil Rights:

> In conclusion . . . I respectfully suggest to you that Judge Carswell is Judge Haynsworth with a cutting edge. He is Judge Haynsworth with a bitterness and a meanness that Judge Haynsworth never had. . . .
>
> You have heard Mr. Pollack (Dean of the Yale Law School) and others say that this man has never written one legal statement for the public. To put in the seat of Oliver Wendell Holmes, who wrote "The Common Law," the seat of Benjamin Cardozo, who wrote "The Nature of the Judicial Process," the seat of Felix Frankfurter, whose writings and scholarship were legion, to put in the seat of those three men a man who has never published one page on the law is to be disrespectful to the great justices of the past. . . .

The negative evidence presented at the Hearings resulted in some Committee members requesting that Carswell be called back and be given the opportunity to refute these allegations. On February 5, the Judiciary Committee voted nine to six not to recall Carswell but invited him to furnish a written rebuttal of the charges made against him. Carswell did so, stating that he had never been hostile to civil rights lawyers and again insisting that he was not a racist.

The Committee then adjourned for one week. Before it reconvened, additional civil right leaders, labor organizations, and law professors went on record as being opposed to the confirmation of Carswell. On February 17, the Judiciary Committee voted thirteen to four to approve the nomination of Carswell. Stories in the newspapers indicated that if the Senate were to immediately begin the debate on whether to confirm Carswell, the proponents would succeed by a narrow margin. It was felt by those in opposition that a delay of the Senate debate would result in additional public opinion being expressed against Carswell.

In addition to the Carswell nomination, the Senate also had before it another contentious matter. This was a Voting Rights Act that was strenuously opposed by many Republican Senators, especially those from the South. Those opposed to Carswell plotted to bring the Voting Rights Act to the Senate before it would consider the Carswell nomination. If they succeeded, then those Senators opposed to the Voting Rights Act who were also in favor of Carswell would be faced with a dilemma. If they filibustered in order to prevent a vote on the Voting Rights Act, Congress would reach its adjournment date without the Senate having the opportunity to vote on the Carswell nomination. If they did not filibuster, the majority of the Senators would not only pass the Voting Rights Act, but those

Senators opposed to Carswell would also obtain their desire to delay the Senate debate on him. After due consideration, the Senate agreed to have the debate and vote on the Voting Rights Act before beginning the debate on the nomination of Carswell. Consequently the Senate did not begin consideration of Carswell's nomination until March 17.

During the interval between the end of the Senate Hearings and the beginning of the Senate debates, further opposition to Carswell did take place. A campaign was started and succeeded in obtaining the signatures of a significant number of Wall Street lawyers on a statement urging the Senate not to confirm Carswell. On March 6, the Ripon Society, an organization of moderate Republican students, released a study in which it charged that Carswell functioned significantly below the level of competency during his many years as a Federal District Judge. It also contained a statistical study that showed that fifty-eight percent of his published decisions were reversed by appellate courts.

Two things occurred at the beginning of the Senate debates that did not bode well for Carswell. First, after one Senator declared that Carswell had an "incredibly undistinguished career," Senator Hruska, a Carswell supporter, made his widely reported remarks that:

> Even if he (Carswell) were mediocre, there are a lot of mediocre judges and people and lawyers. They are entitled to a little representation, aren't they, and a little chance? We can't have all Brandeises and Frankfurters and Cardozos and stuff like that there.

Richard Harris in this book *Decision* called this one of the greatest political blunders in the history of the Senate and an important factor in Carswell's ultimate defeat.

The second occurrence involved Judge E. P. Tuttle, a colleague of Carswell on the Federal Court of Appeals for the Fifth Circuit and an extremely respected jurist. After the nomination of Carswell, Judge Tuttle was asked to support Carswell, and on January 22, 1970, he wrote a letter to the Committee Chairman indicating that he would be willing to appear at the Senate Hearings and testify in Carswell's favor. After the information on Carswell's 1948 racist speech and the Golf Club incident became public, Judge Tuttle then informed Carswell that he would not appear before the Committee to testify in favor of Carswell. On January 28, Governor Collins of Florida appeared before the Judiciary Committee and testified in favor of Carswell. In the course of his testimony (and unaware that Tuttle had told Carswell that he would not testify for him) Collins quoted favorable comments from Judge Tuttle's letter of January 22 and then had the letter placed into the record of the Committee's Proceedings. It was then revealed that Judge Tuttle had sent Carswell a telegram that morning confirming that he would not appear. Carswell was then accused of remaining silent while his supporters used Tuttle's withdrawn endorsement.

The debate on the floor of the Senate began on March 17 and continued for several days, filling many pages of the *Congressional Record*. On March 21, the *New York Times* reported that an unofficial poll of Senators showed forty-five Senators committed or leaning toward Carswell, thirty-seven opposed or leaning against, and sixteen uncommitted. On March 26, the Senate agreed to vote on April 6 on a motion to recommit the nomination back to the Judiciary Committee. Those in favor of such a recommittal did so in the belief that a majority of the Senators would not vote for confirmation. Recommittal would allow the nomination to die in the Judicial Committee, and Senators opposed to Carswell would not have their vote recorded. The Senate voted 51-44 not to recommit.

Meanwhile, additional views of opposition to Carswell were being sent to the Senate. On April 1, 196 former Supreme Court clerks opposed the nominee stating that he had "mediocre ability." On April 4, two members of the American Bar Association Committee confirmed earlier rumors that they had met with Carswell on the night before his first appearance before the Judiciary Committee and had shown him a copy of the Golf Club incorporation papers with his signature on it. It appeared, therefore, that Carswell had given contradictory testimony to the Committee when he testified that he had not been an incorporator.

The final vote came on April 8 and, nearly three months after his name was sent to the Senate and despite the great pressure that the President's Office placed on Republican Senators, the Senate voted 51-45 to reject the appointment of G. Harrold Carswell to become an Associate Justice of the Supreme Court of the United States. President Nixon thus became the first President since 1894 to have two nominations for the Supreme Court rejected by the United States Senate. A bitter President Nixon met the next day with the Press and he spoke against those Senators who had voted against Haynsworth and Carswell. He further said that in his opinion the present Senate would not confirm a Southern conservative to the Supreme Court and that he would look outside of the South for the next candidate.

Despite Nixon's remarks, many commentators stressed that there were many Southern Judges who would have met the President's desire for a conservative and could also have received Senate confirmation without any trouble. In fact, the reasons for the failure of the Senate to confirm were specified in the individual views of the dissenting Senators in the Judiciary Committee Report. These were: Lack of professional competency; Lack of judicial temperament; Refusal to adhere to controlling law in civil rights cases; and Insensitivity to human rights.

On April 14, 1970, President Nixon nominated Harry A. Blackmun of Minnesota to the still vacant seat on the Supreme Court. He was confirmed by the Senate without a dissenting vote.

Shortly after Carswell's rejection, he resigned from the Federal Court of Appeals. The same year he ran for the United States Senate in the Florida Republican primary election and was defeated. He then practiced law in Tallahassee. He died on July 31, 1992, and the *New York Times* in its obituary summed up the clash over the nomination:

> [It] turned into an unusually bitter struggle between the executive and legislative branches. The fight, which was rooted in party politics, ideology and the interplay of pressure groups, culminated in an embarrassing debate of the judge's competence.

Chapter Seventeen

President Ronald W. Reagan
40th President (1981-1989)
Party affiliation: Republican

Supreme Court nomination not confirmed
by the United States Senate:

ROBERT H. BORK
Born: March 1, 1927
Died:
Education: B.A., J.D. University
of Chicago
Nominated Associate Justice,
July 1, 1987
Rejected by Senate,
October 23, 1987

When the Supreme Court of the United States convened on the first Monday in October 1986 for the beginning of its October term, the Court consisted of Chief Justice William H. Rehnquist, age 62; Associate Justices William J. Brennan, age 83; Lewis F. Powell, Jr., age 79; Harry A. Blackmun, age 78; Thurgood Marshall, age 78; Byron R. White, age 69; John Paul Stevens, age 66; Sandra Day O'Connor, age 56; and Antonin Scalia, age 50.

Four Justices -- Rehnquist, O'Connor, Scalia and White -- were considered to be a conservative bloc generally voting against a strict interpretation of separation of church and state, against abortion rights, pro-business and against the extension of civil rights. Justices Blackmun, Brennan, Marshall and Stevens were considered a liberal bloc usually voting opposite of the conservative bloc on similar issues. When these eight Justices were evenly divided, Justice Powell frequently provided the swing vote, sometimes joining the liberal bloc, and on other occasions the conservative bloc.

Chief Justice Rehnquist and Justices O'Connor and Scalia had been appointed by President Reagan. During the 1984 Presidential campaign Reagan made it clear that he would appoint

159

not only conservative Supreme Court justices but only those who would vote to overturn the 1972 case of *Roe v. Wade* which held laws against abortion unconstitutional.

Therefore when Justice Powell on June 26, 1987, the last day of the 1986 October Term, announced his resignation, it became headline news in newspapers and the lead story on network news programs. Although the President was urged to appoint a person with similar views to Justice Powell, both conservatives and liberals seemed to accept the prospect that the President would nominate one who believed in the strict construction of the Constitution. When, in a speech on June 30, Attorney-General Meese said that the administration had no philosophical test for the replacement of the Powell vacancy, many in the audience broke out in laughter.

Five days later, on July 1, 1987, President Reagan announced that he was nominating Robert H. Bork to replace Justice Powell. The next day, the *New York Times* indicated, in a story on the Bork nomination, that his appointment was seen as tipping the ideological balance of the Court to the right, as he would probably provide the critical fifth vote in overturning many of the decisions of the Warren Court.

Since the Presidency of James Madison, constitutional scholars and political scientists have been debating whether the Senate in its constitutional duty of advice and consent should only consider the qualifications of a prospective Supreme Court Justice or should also take into consideration the political philosophy of the nominee. If the Senate were only to consider the qualifications of Bork, there could be no reasonable grounds for not voting to confirm him. He was a graduate of the University of Chicago Law School, had been a partner in two prestigious law firms, a Professor of Constitutional Law at Yale University,

Solicitor-General of the United States, and since 1982 a Judge of the Federal Court of Appeals for the District of Columbia Circuit. He also had published extensively and was generally recognized as one of the leading constitutional theorists.

But unfortunately for Judge Bork, his political and judicial philosophy did concern the Senate and became the focus of the Hearings by the Judiciary Committee and the debates on the floor of the Senate. His consideration by the Senate was the longest and one of the most controversial of all Supreme Court nominees. After his name was sent to the Senate by President Reagan on July 1, 1987, Hearings by the Senate Judiciary Committee did not start until September 15 and lasted for twelve days, with final Senate action occurring October 23, 1987. Articles on the nomination from newspapers, magazines and law reviews during 1987 and 1988 occupy over 100 pages of the printed Hearings. Between 1987 and 1992, four books were published on the Bork confirmation proceedings.

The reason for all of this concern was the writings that Judge Bork had published over his career. He was considered a leading constitutional theorist for the "original intent" interpretation of the Constitution. In brief this theory holds that a judge or justice, in determining whether a particular law is in conflict with the Constitution, must attempt to find the intent of the founders at the time they wrote the Constitution. If the particular right provided for in a law does not appear in the Constitution, then the Court must hold it unconstitutional. To do otherwise will result in the Court making new law rather than interpreting the law. An example of this is the right of privacy. As this is not mentioned anyplace in the Constitution, a state law prohibiting the use of contraceptives by a married couple should not be held unconstitutional by the Supreme Court. Bork over the years had written many articles and given many speeches that criticized earlier Supreme Court decisions on such issues as birth control, abortion, one-person-one-vote, and the poll tax. This led opponents of the original intent theory to claim that Bork's judicial philosophy would not recognize the concept of any rights that were not enumerated in the Constitution.

Immediately after the President's announcement of the Bork nomination, it became apparent that a partisan battle would take place over his confirmation by the Senate. In fact, on the very next day Senator Kennedy made a speech in the Senate in which he declared:

> Robert Bork's America is a land in which women would be forced into back alley abortions, blacks would be segregated at lunch counters . . . school children could not be taught about evolution, writers and artists could be censored at the whim of the government, and the doors of the federal courts would be shut on the fingers for whom the judiciary is -- and is often the only -- protector of the individual rights of our democracy.

At the same time, proponents of Bork were emphasizing his status as a scholar and judge. Between the nomination on July 1 and the beginning of the Judiciary Committee hearings on September 15, both sides began to make plans for obtaining or opposing the confirmation of Judge Bork and for instituting a public relations campaign for public support for their position.

A *U.S. News & World Report* poll published just before the announcement of the nomination showed that 49% believed that a nominee to the Supreme Court should be confirmed even if some Senators disagree with the nominee's ideology. On July 9, at a meeting of civil rights leaders, Senator Joseph Biden,

Chairman of the Senate Judiciary Committee, announced that he would lead the fight to oppose the confirmation of Judge Bork. The next day, the White House accused Senator Biden of politicizing the confirmation process. In the next few days the National Abortion Rights Action League met to plan a national campaign to persuade the Senate not to confirm Judge Bork, while Bork supporters made speeches and wrote letters to newspapers in favor of Bork. On July 30, President Reagan began his campaign to obtain Senate confirmation for Bork and portrayed him as a moderate and reasonable jurist. Beginning in August, both sides commenced broadcasting advertisements, with People for American Way being anti-Bork and the Coalition for America being pro-Bork. Another poll at the beginning of August showed that 50% of the Nation's Judges were in favor of Bork's confirmation.

The American Bar Association's Standing Committee on the Federal Judiciary on September 9 voted to give Judge Bork its highest rating of "well qualified," but four members evaluated him as "not qualified." President Reagan indicated that he was most pleased with this endorsement, while Senator Biden stated that "the most surprising aspect of the vote is that the endorsement was not unanimous." The *New York Times* on September 13 printed a review of Bork's writings and speeches that indicated that Bork had "scornfully repudiated dozens of key Supreme Court decisions expanding individual rights," and these would probably be the basis during his confirmation hearings.

The Senate Judiciary Committee, on September 15, 1987, opened its Hearings on whether or not to confirm the appointment of Robert H. Bork to become an Associate Justice of the Supreme Court of the United States. The Chairman announced that after Judge Bork finished his testimony the Committee would hear panels of academics, judges, representatives of various organizations and other interested citizens. The Hearings were to be televised, and both public and cable television covered the Hearings from gavel to gavel.

Chairman Biden gave his opening statement, and this was followed by Judge Bork's opening statement. The contradictions of judicial philosophy between these two statements became the basis of most of the dialogue between the Committee members and Judge Bork during the next seven days. Biden's opening statement included these remarks:

> We have heard much today about the Bicentennial of the Constitution, but as you and I both know, the Convention in Philadelphia was only one important chapter in the history of our people.... Each generation, in some sense, had been as much the author of our Constitution as the 39 men who affixed their signature to it 200 years ago.

> America is the promised land, because each generation bequeathed to its children a promise that it might not enjoy but which it fully expected their offspring to fulfill. . . . And so, faithful to that tradition . . . the Constitution must become more than an object for celebration -- it is once again to become the center of a critical national debate over what it is and what it must become, especially on where the rights of the individual end and the powers of government begin.

> And so let us make no mistake about the unique importance of this nomination, at this particular moment in our history. . . . So this is no ordinary nomination. In passing on this nomination to the

Supreme Court, we must also pass judgment on whether the nominee's particular philosophy is an appropriate one at this time in our history.

And this is no ordinary nominee. Over more than a quarter-century, Judge Bork has been recognized . . . as *the* leading proponent of a provocative constitutional philosophy. And thus, in a special way, a vote to confirm Judge Bork requires an endorsement of his views as well.

I believe all Americans are born with certain inalienable rights. As a child of God, my rights are not derived from the majority, the state or the Constitution, but they were given to me and each of our fellow citizens by the Creator and represent the essence of human dignity.

After Chairman Biden finished his introductory remarks, Judge Bork presented his statement that included these remarks:

I would like to add a few remarks at the outset on a subject of central interest in this hearing: my understanding of how a judge should go about his or her work. That may also be described as my philosophy of the role of the judge in a constitutional democracy.

The judge's authority derives entirely from the fact that he is applying the law and his [sic] own personal value. . . . No one, including the judge can be above the law. . . .

How should a judge go about finding the law?

The only legitimate way is by attempting to discern what those who made the law intended. The intention of the lawmakers govern whether the lawmakers are the Congress of the United States enacting a statute, or those who ratified our Constitution and its various amendments. Where the words are precise and the facts simple that is a relatively easy task. Where the words are general . . . the task is far more complex -- it is to find the principle or value that was intended to be protected and see that it is protected. . . .

If a judge abandons intention as his guide, there is no law available to him and he begins to legislate a social agenda for the American people. That goes beyond his legitimate authority. He or she diminishes liberty instead of enhancing it. . . .

. . . [W]hen a judge . . . reads entirely new values into the Constitution, values the framers and ratifiers did not put there, he deprives the people of their liberty. That liberty, which the Constitution clearly envisions, is the liberty of the people to set their own social agenda through the process of democracy.

. . . My philosophy of judging is neither liberal or conservative. It is simply a philosophy of judging which gives the Constitution full and fair interpretation but, where the Constitution is silent, leaves the policy struggles to Congress, the President, the legislatures and executives of the fifty states, and to the American people.

The Judiciary committee consisted of thirteen Senators, seven Democrats and six Republicans, each of whom took turns questioning the nominee. The questioning started immediately after Judge Bork's opening statement and continued for five days. Most of the Democratic Senators examined Bork in regard to the various opinions that he had expressed in his past writings and speeches. Did he, they asked, still believe that a state poll tax is constitutional, does the fourteenth amendment only apply to African Americans and not to women, can not a right of privacy be found in the Constitution? These were just a few of their probing questions. Bork in his replies modified his views on some previous positions he had taken on free speech and women's rights and indicated that he would hesitate to overrule cases that he had previously criticized. He asked that he not be judged on his speculative writings as a law professor but rather on his behavior as Solicitor-General and as an appellate court judge. Senator Leahy, when questioned by a reporter about Bork's changing opinions, remarked that they sounded to him like "confirmation conversion."

Most of the Republican Senators used their questions to emphasize Bork's character and qualifications and to support their belief that he was not a radical thinker but was within the main stream of American juridical thought.

The Hearings concluded after the appearance of witnesses including both those in favor of Bork and those against him. On October 7, the Judiciary Committee voted nine to five against giving its consent to the nomination of Judge Bork.

A count of those Senators who had declared that they would vote against Bork made it clear that the Reagan administration did not have the necessary votes for the confirmation of Bork. Several Senators and others requested the

President to recall his name. But to the surprise of many, on October 9, Judge Bork declared that he would not ask the President to withdraw his name although he realized that he had little chance to be confirmed by the Senate.

The Judiciary Committee issued its Report to the Senate on October 13. The Report, which contained 407 pages, set forth the reasons why the majority members voted not to recommend the confirmation of Judge Bork as well as the reasons of those members who voted for Bork's confirmation.

The Majority Report noted that although the American Bar Association's Standing Committee on the Federal Judiciary had voted that Judge Bork was "well qualified," its highest rating, the Committee was concerned that one member voted "opposed" and four "not qualified." The Report pointed out that the Judiciary Committee had never approved a nominee who had received even one "unqualified" vote. The remainder of the Majority Report expressed their belief that Judge Bork's position on civil rights, first amendment rights, and on the right of privacy were such that it concluded that:

> His jurisprudence fails to incorporate the ennobling concepts of the Constitution. It is thus fundamentally at odds with the express understanding of the Framers and with the history of the Supreme Court in building our traditions of constitutionalism. By depriving the Constitution of its spirit, that philosophy threatens the vitality of our tradition. Above all, our nation demands that the Supreme Court exercise wisdom and statesmanship in mediating conflicts spurred by growth and change in a dynamic society.

The Minority Report replied to all of the criticism in the Majority Report and concluded that:

As [our] views indicate, Judge Bork is eminently qualified by ability, and experience to serve as Associate Justice of the Supreme Court. The failure of the Senate to confirm will be a failure larger than simply denying one qualified nominee a place on the Court. It will be a disservice to the process by rewarding those who have turned the nominating process into a negative campaign of distortions; it will be a disservice to the judiciary of this country who should not be forced to endure such a politicized process; and most importantly, it will be a disservice to the American people, who not only will be denied the service of this intellect on the Court, but will also see the judiciary have its independence threatened by activist special interest groups.

The campaign for or against Judge Bork outside of the Senate continued at a hectic pace. The White House and the Justice Department continued to put pressure on those Senators who had not as yet announced how they would vote. President Reagan made several speeches in support of Bork. Special interest groups on both sides held fund-raising affairs and millions of dollars were spent on radio, television and newspaper advertising. The coalition of civil rights and women's organizations out-spent the pro-Bork coalition of conservative organizations and many of their advertisements contained exaggerations and some misstatements about Judge Bork's beliefs. The active participation of special interest groups in the process of the confirmation of Supreme Court nominees, that began with the nomination of Judge Parker in 1930, increased with the

Haynsworth-Carswell nominations in 1969 and 1970 and reached full flower in the Bork nomination. Never before had the mass media been so successfully utilized.

The nomination of Judge Bork as Associate Justice of the Supreme Court finally reached the floor of the Senate nearly four months after President Reagan sent his name to the Senate. Although over fifty Senators had already stated that they would vote against confirmation, Senators in favor of Bork attempted to shift the focus of the debate from Bork's record to the tactics used by the opposition. On October 23, the Senate voted 58-42 against the confirmation of Judge Bork, with six Republicans joining the majority and two Democrats joining the minority. This was the largest margin by which any Supreme Court nominee had ever been defeated. Although those in favor of Judge Bork agreed with President Reagan's statement after the Senate vote that a campaign of "political pressure" caused the defeat of the nomination, most commentators agreed that Bork was the cause of his own undoing by having constitutional theories that differed from those of most Americans who had come to expect a broader right of privacy. An interesting aspect of the Senate vote is that nearly all of the Senators from the South voted against the confirmation. This reflected the increased voting power of the Southern Blacks whose support was the deciding factor in those Senators being elected.

Despite President Reagan's threat that if Bork was defeated he would nominate a candidate that would "upset the Democrats as much as Judge Bork does," on November 30, 1987, he nominated Anthony M. Kennedy, a Judge on the Federal Court of Appeals for the Ninth Circuit. Judge Kennedy was a more moderate conservative than Judge Bork, and on February 3, 1988, he was confirmed by a vote of 93-0.

Chapter Eighteen

Other Nominations

Of the twenty-seven nominations to the Supreme Court that were not confirmed by the Senate, the first was that of Senator William Paterson who was nominated by President George Washington on February 27, 1793, to fill a vacant seat for an Associate Justice. Washington withdrew his name the next day when it was realized that Senator Paterson was still a member of the Congress that enacted the Judicial Act of 1789 which had created the Court positions. Consequently, Paterson was not eligible for an appointment to the Court. As soon as Paterson's term as Senator in the first Congress expired on March 4, 1793, President Washington again submitted his name to the Senate, which confirmed him on the same day. As his rejection by the Senate was only on a technicality, and as the Senate confirmed as soon as legally possible, he is not included in these *Sketches*.

Edward King twice failed to receive confirmation by the Senate. He was first nominated by President Tyler, but the Senate postponed taking any action. As soon as the new Congress convened, Tyler submitted his name again but then withdrew it when it became apparent that the Senate still would not confirm him. Therefore, the sketches of twenty-six men are included in this volume. Two men originally not confirmed were

171

subsequently nominated again and confirmed. These were Roger Taney and Stanley Matthews.

There were also seven instances when nominees were confirmed by the Senate but then declined the appointment. Before the Presidency of Martin Van Buren starting in 1837, it was customary to send the names of nominees to the Senate without consulting the nominees. Presumably this was done because of the slowness of communications in the early days of the Republic.

The only instance of a later President sending a name to the Senate without first receiving the consent of the nominee occurred in 1882, when President Arthur tried to convince Roscoe Conkling, a prominent New York politician, to agree to his nomination. Conkling told the President that he did not wish to become a Supreme Court Justice. President Arthur sent his name to the Senate anyway with the belief that Conkling would accept the appointment once the Senate confirmed his nomination. But Conkling held his ground and declined the appointment. According to contemporary newspaper accounts, Conkling rejected the appointment because he planned to run for President.

The seven men who declined appointment to the Supreme Court after receiving confirmation by the Senate were:

Robert Harrison, 1789
William Cushing (for Chief Justice), 1796
John Jay (for Chief Justice), 1800
Levi Lincoln, 1811
John Quincy Adams, 1811
William Smith, 1837
Roscoe Conkling, 1882

Appendix I

CHART

Nominee	President	Party of President	Date of Nomination
John Rutledge	G. Washington	Fed.	7/01/1795
Alexander Wolcott	J. Madison	Dem-Rep	2/04/1811
John J. Crittenden	J. Q. Adams	Dem-Rep	12/17/1828
Roger B. Taney	A. Jackson	Dem.	1/15/1835
John C. Spencer Reuben H. Walworth Edward King Edward King John M. Read	J. Tyler	Whig	1/09/1844 3/13/1844 6/05/1844 12/04/1844 2/07/1845
George W. Woodward	J. K. Polk	Dem.	11/23/1845
Edward A. Bradford George E. Badger William C. Micou	M. Fillmore	Whig	8/16/1852 1/10/1853 2/24/1853
Jeremiah S. Black	J. Buchanan	Dem.	2/05/1861
Henry Stanbery	A. Johnson	Dem.	4/16/1866
Ebenezer R. Hoar George H. Williams Caleb Cushing	U. S. Grant	Rep.	12/15/1869 12/01/1873 1/09/1874
Stanley Matthews	R. B. Hayes	Rep.	1/26/1881
William B. Hornblower Wheeler H. Peckham	G. Cleveland	Dem.	9/19/1893 1/22/1894
John J. Parker	H. C. Hoover	Rep.	3/21/1930
Abe Fortas Homer Thornberry	L. B. Johnson	Dem.	6/26/1968 6/26/1968
Clement Haynsworth G. Harrold Carswell	R. M. Nixon	Rep.	8/18/1969 1/19/1970
Robert H. Bork	R. W. Reagan	Rep.	7/01/1987

Senate Action	Senate Composition	Supreme Court Seat Filled by
Rejected 14-10, 12/15/1795	Fed=19, Anti-Fed=13	Oliver Ellsworth
Rejected 24-9, 2/13/1811	Dem-Rep=28, Fed=6	Joseph Story
Postponed 2/12/1829	D-Rep=28, N-Rep=20	John McLean
Postponed 3/03/1835	Dem=20, Whigs=20	Philip P. Barbour
Rejected 26-21, 1/31/1844 Withdrawn, 6/17/1844 Postponed, 6/15/1844 Withdrawn, 2/07/1845 No action	Whigs=28, Dem=25	Samuel Nelson
Rejected 29-20, 1/22/1846	Dem=31, Whigs=25	Robert C. Grier
No Action Postponed, 2/11/1853 No Action	Dem=35, Whigs=24	John A. Campbell
Rejected 26-25, 2/21/1861	Dem=36, Rep=26	Samuel F. Miller
No Action	Rep=36, Dem=26	Seat eliminated*
Rejected 33-24, 2/03/1870 Withdrawn, 1/08/1874 Withdrawn, 1/13/1874	Rep=56, Dem=11	Joseph P. Bradley Morrison R. Waite
No Action	Dem=42, Rep=38	Stanley Matthews**
Rejected 30-24, 1/15/1894 Rejected 41-32, 2/16/1894	Dem=44, Rep=38	Edward D. White
Rejected 41-39, 5/07/1930	Rep=56, Dem=39	Owen J. Roberts
Withdrawn, 10/04/1968 Withdrawn, 10/04/1968	Dem=64, Rep=36	***
Rejected 55-45, 11/21/1969 Rejected 51-45, 4/08/1970	Dem=58, Rep=42	Harry Blackmun
Rejected 58-42, 10/23/1987	Dem=55, Rep=45	Anthony M. Kennedy

*   Congress in 1866 provided for the reduction of Supreme Court seats to 7 as vacancies occurred; thus, this seat was not filled.

** Matthews' name was resubmitted by President Arthur, who became President after the death of President Garfield.

*** Chief Justice Warren had submitted his resignation "effective upon confirmation of his successor," and as Fortas' name was withdrawn, Warren remained as Chief Justice and no vacancy was available for Thornberry.

Appendix II

SOURCES

Chapter Two

Henry J. Abraham, *Justices and Presidents: A Political History of Appointments to the Supreme Court of the United States*, 3rd Ed., 1992.

Dictionary of American Biography

Encyclopedia Britannica (for Jay Treaty)

Henry Flanders, *The Lives and Times of the Chief Justices of the United States*, 1881.

Leon Friedman and Fred Israel, *The Justices of the United States Supreme Court: Their Lives and Major Opinions, 1789-1969*, Vol. I, 1969.

Joseph P. Harris, *The Advice and Consent of the Senate: A Study of the Confirmation of Appointments by the United States Senate*, 1953.

Thomas Jefferson, *The Writings of Thomas Jefferson*, Collected and edited by Paul L. Ford, Vol. VII, 1896 (letter of March 2, 1796)

S. McCowan, "Chief Justice Rutledge and the Jay Treaty," *The South Carolina Historical Magazine*, 62:10, 1961.

178

George Van Santwoord, *Sketches of the Lives, Times, and Judicial Services of the Chief Justices of the United States: Jay, Rutledge, Ellsworth, Marshall, Taney, and Waite.* Rev. Ed. 1882.
Charles Warren, *The Supreme Court in United States History,* Rev. Ed., Vol. I, 1932.

Chapter Three

Columbian Centinel, February 1811.

Connecticut Courant, February 1811.

Dictionary of American Biography

Irving Brant, *A History of Connecticut: Its People and Institutions,* 1914.

Franklin B. Dexter, *Biographical Sketches of the Graduates of Yale College with Anals of the College History,* Vol. IV, 1907.

Joseph P. Harris, *The Advice and Consent of the Senate: A Study of the Confirmation of Appointments by the United States Senate,* 1953.

New York Evening Post, February 1811.

Peter Percess, *Connecticut in Transition,* 1918.

Charles Warren, *The Supreme Court in United States History,* Vol. I, 1789-1821; 1927.

Chapter Four

Ann M. Coleman, *The Life of John Crittenden, with Selections from His Correspondence and Speeches,* Vol. I, 1871.

Calvin Colton, *The Private Correspondence of Henry Clay*, 1856.

James Marquis, *Andrew Jackson, Portrait of a President*, 1937.

Edward Pessen, *Jacksonian America, Personality, and Politics*, Rev. Ed., 1985.

Robert Scigiano, *Supreme Court and the Presidency*, 1971.

Charles Warren, *The Supreme Court in United States History*, Rev. Ed., Vol. I, 1932.

Chapter Five

Don Fehrenbacher, *The Dred Scott Case: Its Significance in American Law and Politics*, 1978.

Leon Friedman and Fred Israel, *The Justices of the United States Supreme Court: Their Lives and Major Opinions, 1789-1969*, Vol. I, 1969.

Joseph Harris, *The Advice and Consent of the Senate: A Study of the Confirmation of Appointments by the United States Senate*, 1953.

Walker F. Lewis, *Without Fear or Favor, A Biography of Chief Justice Roger Brooke Taney*, 1965.

Bernar C. Steiner, *Life of Roger Brooke Taney , Chief Justice of the United States Supreme Court*, 1922.

Carl B. Swisher, *Roger B. Taney*, 1935.

S. Tyler, *Memoir of Roger Brooke Taney, LL.D., Chief Justice of the Supreme Court of the United States*, 1872.

George Van Santwoord, *Sketches of the Lives, Times, and Judicial Services of the Chief Justices of the United States: Jay,*

Rutledge, Ellsworth, Marshall, Taney, and Waite, Rev. Ed, 1882.

Charles Warren, *The Supreme Court in United States History*, Rev. Ed., Vol. I, 1932.

Washington Post, February 11, 1835.

Chapter Six

Henry J. Abraham, *Justices and Presidents: A Political History of Appointments to the Supreme Court of the United States*, 3rd Ed., 1992.

Dictionary of American Biography.

Cortex A. Ewing, *The Judges of the Supreme Court, 1789-1937: A Study of Their Qualifications*, 1938.

The Legal Intelligencer, May 16, 1873 (Obituary for Edward King); December 11, 1874 (Obituary for John M. Read).

John Livingstone, *Portraits of Eminent Americans Now Living*, Vol. II, 1853.

Pittsburgh Legal Journal, December 9, 1874.

Nathan Sargent, *Public Men and Events from the Commencement of Mr. Monroe's Administration in 1817 to the Close of Mr. Fillmore's Administration*, Vol. II, 1875.

William W. Story, *Life and Letters of Joseph Story*, Vol. VII, 1851.

Irving Browne, "Rueben Hyde Walworth," *The Green Bag*, Vol. III, June 1895.

Charles Warren, *The Supreme Court in United States History*, Rev. Ed., Vol. II, 1935.

Chapter Seven

Henry J. Abraham, *Justices and Presidents: A Political History of Appointments to the Supreme Court of the United States*, 3rd Ed., 1992.

Paul H. Bergeron, *The Presidency of James K. Polk*, 1987.

David P. Brown, *The Forum; Forty Years of Full Practice at the Philadelphia Bar*, Vol. II, 1856.

Dictionary of American Biography.

Alvin Nevins, Ed., *Polk, The Diary of a President, 1845-1849*, 1929.

New York Herald, January-February, 1846.

Charles Warren, *The Supreme Court in United States History*, Rev. Ed., Vol. II, 1935.

Chapter Eight

Henry J. Abraham, *Justices and Presidents: A Political History of Appointments to the Supreme Court of the United States*, 3rd Ed., 1992.

Dictionary of American Biography.

Eli N. Evans, *Judah P. Benjamin*, 1988.

William A. Graham, *Discourse in Memory of the Life and Character of the Hon. Geo. E. Badger, Delivered ... at Raleigh, July 19, 1866*, 1866.

Joseph P. Harris, *The Advice and Consent of the Senate: A Study of the Confirmation of Appointments by the United States Senate*, 1953.

The Legal Intelligencer, May 14, 1875.

New York Daily Tribune, January 8, 1853.

New York Daily Times, January 14, February 12, 16, 1853.

Robert Scigiano, *The Supreme Court and the Presidency*, 1971.

Charles Warren, *The Supreme Court in United States History*, Rev. Ed., Vol. II, 1935.

Chapter Nine

Chancery F. Black, *Essays and Speeches of Jeremiah S. Black, With a Biographical Sketch*, 1880.

William M. Brigance, *Jeremiah N. Sullivan Black: A Defender of the Court and the Constitution*, 1934.

Dictionary of American Biography.

Charles Warren, *The Supreme Court in United States History*, Rev. Ed., Vol. II, 1935.

Chapter Ten

Henry J. Abraham, *Justices and Presidents: A Political History of Appointments to the Supreme Court of the United States*, 3rd Ed., 1992.

The Albany Law Review, Vol. 34:317, 1886-1887.

Howard K. Beale, *Diary of Gideon Welles*, Vol. II, 1960.

The Congressional Globe, July 18, 1886.

Dictionary of American Biography.

Charles Fairman, *Reconstruction and Union, 1864-88*, Vol. II, Part I: The Oliver Wendell Holmes Devise, 1987.

Ransome H. Gillet, *Democracy in the United States. What it Has Done, What it is Doing, and What it Will Do*, 1886.

The Philadelphia Inquirer, April 18, 1866.

W. Swindler, "The Politics of Advice and Consent," *American Bar Association Journal*, June 1970.

Charles Warren, *The Supreme Court in United States History*, Rev. Ed., Vol. II, 1935.

Chapter Eleven

Henry J. Abraham, *Justices and Presidents: A Political History of Appointments to the Supreme Court of the United States*, 3rd Ed, 1992.

American Law Review, Vol. 4:380, 1870.

Cortex A. Ewing, *The Judges of the Supreme Court, 1789-1937: A Study of Their Qualifications*, 1938.

Dictionary of American Biography.

Harper's Weekly, January 1, 1870.

John P. Frank, "The Appointment of Supreme Court Justices and Politics, I" *Wisconsin Law Review*, 1941.

Joseph P. Harris, *The Advice and Consent of the Senate: A Study of the Confirmation of Appointments by the United States Senate*, 1953.

George Hoar, *Autobiography of Seventy Years*, Vol. II, 1903.

The Nation, December 2, 1869; January 6, 1870.

184

New York Times, December 12 and 25, 1869.

James Schouler, *History of the Reconstruction Period, 1865-1877*, Vol. VII, 1913.

Moorfield Storey and Edward W. Emerson, *Ebenezer Rockwood Hoar: A Memoir*, 1911.

Laurence H. Tribe, *God Save This Honorable Court: How the Choice of Supreme Court Justices Shapes Our History*, 1985.

Charles Warren, *The Supreme Court in United States History*, Rev. Ed., Vol. II, 1935.

Chapter Twelve

Henry J. Abraham, *Justices and Presidents: A Political History of the Appointments to the Supreme Court of the United States*, 3rd Ed., 1992.

John P. Frank, "The Appointment of Supreme Court Justices and Politics, II," *Wisconsin Law Review*, 1941.

Richard D. Friedman, "The Transformation in Senate Response to Supreme Court Nominations: From Reconstruction to the Taft Administration and Beyond," *Cardozo Law Review*, Vol. 5, 1983.

Harold M. Helfman, "The Contested Confirmation of Stanley Matthews to the Supreme Court," *Bulletin of the Historical and Philosophical Society of Ohio*, Vol. 8, 1950.

William D. Draper, *Great American Lawyers: A History of the Legal Profession in America*, 1909.

New York Times, January 27, 30, February 2, 8, 9, 10, April 4, 11, May 13, 1881.

New York Tribune, January 28, 1881.

Chapter Thirteen

American Law Review, Vol. 28, January-February 1894.

Henry J. Abraham, *Justices and Presidents: A Political History of Appointments to the Supreme Court of the United States*, 3rd Ed., 1992.

Benjamin N. Cardozo, *Association of the Bar of New York: Yearbook*, 1915:187.

Dictionary of American Biography.

Allan Nevins, *Grover Cleveland, A Study in Courage*, 1932.

New York State Bar Association: *Proceedings*, Twenty-Eighth Annual Meeting, 1915.

New York Times, January 23, 1894.

New York Tribune, October 7, 1893; January 23, 25, February 17, 1894.

Carl A. Pierce, *A Vacancy on the Supreme Court: The Politics of Judicial Appointment*, 1893-94.

Chapter Fourteen

Henry J. Abraham, *Justices and Presidents: A Political History of Appointments to the Supreme Court of the United States*, 3rd Ed., 1992.

Frederick L. Allen, *Only Yesterday*. 1931.

Congressional Record, Vol. 72, 1930.

Peter J. Fish, "Red Jacket Revisited: The Case That Unraveled John J. Parker's Supreme Court Appointment," *Law & History Review*, Vol. 5, 1987.

John P. Frank, "The Appointment of Supreme Court Justices and Politics, III," *Wisconsin Law Review*, 1941.

Paul A. Freund, "Appointment of Justices: Some Historical Perspectives," *Harvard Law Review*, Vol. 110, 1988.

Joel B. Grossman & Stephen Wasby, "Haynsworth and Parker, History Does Live Again," *South Carolina Law Review*, Vol. 23, 1971.

Joseph P. Harris, *The Advice and Consent of the Senate: A Study of the Confirmation of Appointments by the United States Senate*, 1953.

Dariene C. Hines, "The NAACP and the Supreme Court: Walter F. White and the Defeat of John J. Parker," *Negro History Bulletin*, Vol. 40, 1977.

Herbert Hoover, *The Memoirs of Herbert Hoover: The Cabinet and the Presidency, 1920-1932*, Vol. II, 1952.

Roy M. Mersky & J. Myron Jacobstein, *The Supreme Court of the United States: Hearings and Reports on Successful and Unsuccessful Nominations of Supreme Court Justices by the Senate Judiciary Committee, 1916-1975*, Vol. 9, 1977.

Merlo J. Pusey, *Charles Evans Hughes*, Vol. II, 1951.

Richard L. Watson, "The Defeat of Judge Parker: A Study in Pressure Groups and Politics," *The Mississippi Valley Historical Review*, Vol. 50, 1963.

Chapter Fifteen

Congressional Record, July, September 1968.

Robert A. Caro, *Means of Ascent*, 1990.

Robert Dallek, *Lone Star Rising: Lyndon Johnson and His Times, 1908-1960*, 1991.

Leon Friedman & Fred Israel, *The Justices of the United States Supreme Court: Their Lives and Major Opinions, 1789-1969*, Vol. IV, 1969.

Alpheus T. Mason, "Pyrrhic Victory: The Defeat of Abe Fortas," *The Virginia Quarterly Review*, Vol. 19, 1969.

John Massaro, "LBJ and the Fortas Nomination for Chief Justice," *Political Science Quarterly*, 1982.

Roy M. Mersky and J. Myron Jacobstein, *The Supreme Court of the United States: Hearings and Reports on Successful and Unsuccessful Nominations of Supreme Court Justices by the Senate Judiciary Committee, 1916-1975*, Vol. 7, 9A, 1977.

Bruce A. Murphy, *Fortas, The Rise and Fall of a Supreme Court Justice*, 1988.

Robert Shogan, *A Question of Judgment: The Fortas Case and the Struggle for the Supreme Court*, 1972.

Chapter Sixteen

Henry J. Abraham, *Justices and Presidents: A Political History of Appointments to the Supreme Court of the United States*, 3rd Ed., 1992.

Congressional Record, March, April, November 1970.

188

Richard Harris, *Decision*, 1971.

Roy M. Mersky & J. Myron Jacobstein, *The Supreme Court of the United States: Hearings and Reports on Successful and Unsuccessful Nominations of Supreme Court Justices by the Senate Judiciary Committee, 1916-1975*, Vol. 10-11, 1977.

Herbert S. Parmet, *Richard Nixon and His America*, 1990.

Chapter Seventeen

Robert Bork, *The Tempting of America: The Political Seduction of the Law*, 1990.

Ethan Bronner, *Battle for Justice: How the Bork Nomination Shook America*, 1989.

Congressional Record, September, October 1987.

Mark Gitenstein, *Matters of Principle: An Insider's Account of America's Rejection of Robert Bork's Nomination to the Supreme Court*, 1992.

Roy M. Mersky & J. Myron Jacobstein, *The Supreme Court of the United States: Hearings and Reports on Successful and Unsuccessful Nominations of Supreme Court Justices by the Senate Judiciary Committee, 1916-1987*, Vols. 14, 14E, 1990.

Patrick B. McGuigan & Dawn M. Weyrich, *Ninth Justice, The Fight for Bork; with an Analysis of Media Coverage by R. H. Bork, Jr., and the Judicial Notice Interview with Judge Robert H. Bork*, 1990.

New York Times, September, October 1987.

Michael Pertschuk & Wendy Schaetzel, *The People Rising: The Campaign Against the Bork Nomination*, 1989.